BATTANI

DOVEL

The Ancestors of
Charles Darnbrook Colson
Quinn Higgins Colson
Jacob Michael Dovel and
Dakota Orion Dovel

Compiled and Edited by
Stanton Darnbrook Colson

BATTANI

DOVEL

The Ancestors of
Charles Darnbrook Colson
Quinn Higgins Colson
Jacob Michael Dovel and
Dakota Orion Dovel

Compiled and Edited by
Stanton Darnbrook Colson

ISBN 13: 978-1518880414
ISBN 10: 151888041X

*Published by AAS White Heron Press
1623 Soundneck Road, Elizabeth City, NC 27909
White Heron Press and associated logos are trademarks
and/or
registered trademarks of American Artists' Studios*

Printed in the U.S.A.

Cover Design by Kim Colson

This Book
Chronicles the
Battani and Dovel Families
The Ancestors of
Charles Darnbrook Colson
Quinn Higgins Colson
Jacob Michael Dovel and
Dakota Orion Dovel

[Additional photographs, documents
and research for this book are on file
with Stanton Darnbrook Colson]

Please feel free to send any corrections,
changes and/or updates to the editor
at the email address provided below.

Stanton Darnbrook Colson
cwaveofobx@yahoo.com

Acknowledgments

Thanks to those who assisted in providing information and photographs for this book, including Chris Colson, Elizabeth Ann Battani Colson, Kay Battani, Clara Battani Sertich and Tina Snider

Dedicated to

Wanda Altizer Dovel Mason

Brief Foreword
from the Editor

The research for this book has been ongoing for several years, and and will continue well after this work has been published. Family history is an ongoing, never-ending project. With that in mind, at the back of this volume I have created an addenda page where the reader may insert the appropriate page number and any comment/correction/updates, etc. I would also encourage the reader to forward this information to me at the email address provided at the beginning of this book.

The Battani Family

Elizabeth with (Top to Bottom)
Dakota, Jacob, Quinn and
Charles (in lap)

The Life and Times of
Elizabeth Ann[3] Battani

PATERNAL ANCESTRY: [BATTANI: Charles Anton[2], Theodore Joseph[1] "Tito," Camillo[1a] "Charles," Ricardo[2a], Luigi[3a]]

MATERNAL ANCESTRY: [BENNETT: Kathryn Aileen "Kay," Tilford Oliver Monroe "Tom," Al]

ELIZABETH ANN[3] was born on August 31, 1972 at San Jose, Santa Clara County, California. Her father was Charles Anton[2] Battani of Madrid, Boone County, Iowa. Her mother was Kathryn Aileen "Kay" Bennett of San Francisco, California.

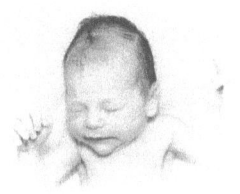

Elizabeth at Birth

ELIZABETH ANN[3] graduated from Broad Run High School, Sterling, Loudoun County, Virginia. She and her first husband, Ronald[8], lived in a variety of locations during his job changes, including Stephens City, Virginia, Mundspark, Arizona, Sacramento, California, Rio Linda, California, Tallahassee, Alabama, Gulfport, Mississippi and Reno, Washoe County, Nevada where their second child, Jacob Michael[9] was born.

ELIZABETH ANN[3] married, first, Ronald Hilton[8] Dovel on May 25, 1991 at Great Falls, Fairfax County, Virginia. They were divorced on August 11, 1997 at Statesville, Iredell County, North Carolina. Ronald[8] was born on June 30, 1964 at Winchester, Frederick County, Virginia. His father was Richard Harvey[7] [Carl Sylvester[6] {of Stanley, Page County, Virginia}, William Tazewell[5] {of East Liberty, Page County, Virginia}, Peter Simon[4], William[3] {of Alma, Rockingham County, Virginia}, David S.[2], Jr., David S.[1] {of England and later of Ingham, Rockingham County, Virginia}] Dovel of Stephens City, Frederick County, Virginia. His mother was Wanda Jean[8] [Roy Cecil Riley[7], William Fulton[6] {of Indian Creek, Tazwell County, Virginia}, Riley A.[5] {of Harmon, Tazwell County, Virginia}, William A.[4] {of Montgomery County, Virginia}, David Riley[3], Emera[2] {of Dutchess County, New York}, Johan Peter[1] {Althauser of Segendorff, Germany}, Wilmhelm[1a], Jacob[2a]] Altizer of Tazwell County, Virginia. Wanda Jean[8] married, second, Harvey L. DeSchon. She married, third, David A. Mason [see the file on Richard Harvey[7] Dovel for details].

Ronald Hilton[8] Dovel had married, first, Sharon Lynn "Sheri" Westover on January 3, 1984 at Winchester, Frederick County, Virginia. They were divorced on May 2, 1991 at Winchester, Frederick County, Virginia. She was born on September 15, 1953 in West

Virginia. Her father was Don Alden Westover of Frederick County, Virginia. Her mother was Betty Leadbetter. Ronald[8] and Sheri had one child: Katie Lynn[9].

Sharon married, second, Philip Lee McBride on November 1, 2005 at Winchester, Frederick County, Virginia. Issue, if any, is not known.

Ronald Hilton[8] Dovel married, third, Debra "Debi" Coffman on May 12, 2000 at Winchester, Frederick County, Virginia by the Justice of the Peace. She was born on August 3, 1957 in Frederick County, Virginia. Her father was Allen Eldridge Coffman of Virginia. Her mother was Elsie Williams of Arkansas. Ronald[8] and Debi had no issue [Editor's Note: However, he is raising her children and one grandchild by Debi's first marriage]. Ronald[8] and Debi currently [2015] live at Inwood, Berkeley County, West Virginia. Ronald[8] and Debi had no issue.

Debi married, first, (Unknown) Fries. Debi and (Unknown) Fries had four children: Matthew, Mary, Bridgett and Sarah.

ELIZABETH ANN[3] married, second, Christopher Philip[11] Colson on September 16, 1997 at Statesville, Iredell County, North Carolina. Elizabeth[3] and Christopher[11] were divorced on June 30, 2005 in

Pasquotank County, North Carolina. He was born on July 6, 1970 in the Calambrone Military Hospital at Pisa, Tuscany, Italy. His biological father was Philip Alan[5] [Leo Francis[4], Oscar Joseph[3], Ernest Albert[2], William[1] {of England}, (Mary[1a] or Sarah[1a]), George[2a], Friend[3a]] Coleman of Landover, Prince Georges County, Maryland. His adoptive father was Stanton Darnbrook[10] [Douglas Herman[9], Henry Wilson[8], Stanton E(phraim)[7], Theophilus T.[6] 2nd, Ephraim[5], Ichabod Downs[4], Hatevil[3], Samuel[2], Cornelius[1], Jan Cornelissen[1a] Van Rotterdam {of Rotterdam, The Netherlands}, Cornelius Jonckers[2a]] Colson of Cambridge, Middlesex County, Massachusetts. His mother was Donna Marie[5] [Robert Charles[4], Joseph Francis[3], John Joseph[2], John[1] {of Ireland}] Higgins of Washington, D. C.

ELIZABETH ANN[3] married, third, Wolfgang[1] Murlebach on October 18, 2014 at Port St. Lucie, St. Lucie County, Florida in the County Clerk of the Circuit Court Annex. Wolfgang[1] was born on March 9, 1966 in Germany. The name of his father and mother is not known.

Wolfgang[1] had married, first, Maria Nella Ortiz. Their divorce was recorded on March 15, 2010 at Stuart, Stuart County, Florida.

ELIZABETH ANN[3] was living with friends in Sterling Park, Loudoun County, Virginia when she met her second husband, Christopher[11]. Elizabeth[3], Christopher[11] and her two sons moved to Statesville, Iredale County, North Carolina, where they were later married. In 2001 the family moved to Weeksville, Pasquotank County, North Carolina. In 2004 she graduated from the College of the Albemarle with an associates degree in Medical Technology and shortly thereafter began work as a Operating Room Surgical Technician at the Albemarle Hospital at Elizabeth City, Pasquotank County, North Carolina.

ELIZABETH ANN[3] received her Associate Degree in Nursing from the College of the Albemarle in May 2009. She currently resides [2015] with her third husband at Port St. Lucie, St. Lucie County, Florida.

The Children of
Elizabeth Ann[3] Battani
and Ronald Hilton[8] Dovel

1. Dakota Orion[9] Dovel
   born on December 14. 1992 in the Reston Hospital Center at Reston, Fairfax County, Virginia. He married Erica Christine McPhee on June 19, 2015 at the Norfolk Botanical Gardens at Norfolk, Hampton Roads, Virginia. Erica was born on October 3, 1991 at Virginia Beach, Hampton Roads, Virginia.

Her father was Eric Christopher McPhee of Norfolk, Hampton Roads, Virginia. Her mother was Judy Lynn Scarbro of Virginia Beach, Hampton Roads, Virginia. Dakota[9] graduated [June 2010] from Northeastern High School at Elizabeth City, Pasquotank County, North Carolina, where he participated all four years in the NHS Air Force Jr. ROTC program, finishing up as President of the Cadet Program and Cadet Lt. Colonel. As of 2015, Dakota and Erica were living at Virginia Beach, Hampton Roads, Virginia.

2. Jacob Michael[9] Dovel
   born on February 18, 1996 at Reno, Washoe County, Nevada. In 2007 and 2008 he was a member of the River Road Middle School golf team. In 2009/2010 he attended the 9th and 10th grades at Northeastern High School at Elizabeth City, Pasquotank County, North Carolina, where he was a member of the Air Force Jr. ROTC program and was a member of the golf team. In 2011 he moved with his mother to Port St. Lucie, St. Lucie County, Florida, graduating in June 2013 from St. Lucie High School, where he finished as a Cadet Lt. Colonel in the Army Jr. ROTC program. In August 2013 he enlisted in the United States Air Force and is currently [2015] stationed at Moody Air Force Base at Valdosta, Lowndes County, Georgia as a maintenance assistant crew chief for

the A-10 Warthog ground support aircraft. Jacob[9] is currently [2015] engaged to Cadlynne Dunhill and they are planning a Spring 2016 wedding at Port St. Lucie, St. Lucie County, Florida.

The Children of
Elizabeth Ann[3] Battani
and Christopher Philip[11] Colson

3. Quinn Higgins[12] Colson
   born on September 13, 1999 at 5:21 am at Iredell Memorial Hospital at Statesville, Iredale County, North Carolina, Doctor Susan Roque, M.D. attending. From 2006 thru 2010 Quinn[12] attended kindergarten through the 4th grade at Weeksville Elementary School at Weeksville, Pasquotank County, North Carolina. In 2011 he attended the 5th grade at J. C. Sawyer Elementary at Elizabeth City, Pasquotank County, North Carolina. In August 2011 he moved with his mother to Port St. Lucie, St. Lucie County, Florida where through 2014 he attended the 6th through the 8th grades at Southport Middle School. In the fall of 2014 he attended the 9th grade at Treasure Coast High School where he is currently [2015] in the 10th grade.

4. Charles Darnbrook[12] Colson
   born on November 15, 2001 at the Albemarle Hospital, Elizabeth City, Pasquotank County,

North Carolina, Doctor Daniel P. Dwyer, attending. From 2008 through 2010 Charles[12] attended kindergarten through the 2nd grade at Weeksville Elementary School at Weeksville, Pasquotank County, North Carolina. In 2011 he attended the 3rd grade at J. C. Sawyer Elementary at Elizabeth City, Pasquotank County, North Carolina. In August 2011 he moved with his mother to Port St. Lucie, St. Lucie County, Florida where through 2013 he attended the 4th and 5th grades at Mariposa Elementary School. From 2013 through 2014 he attended the 6th and 7th grades at Southport Middle School. He currently [2015] attends the 8th grade at Westgate Middle School in St. Lucie County, Florida.

Charles Anton Battani, Elizabeth Ann Battani
and Kathryn Aileen "Kay" {Bennett} Battani

The Life and Times of
Charles Anton[2] Battani

PATERNAL ANCESTRY: [BATTANI: Theodore Joesph[1] "Tito," Camillo[1a] "Charles," Ricardo[2a], Luigi[3a]]

MATERNAL ANCESTRY: [MATTHEIA/ MATAYA: Anna Mary[2], Anton[1] "Anthony/Tony," Simon[1a]]

CHARLES ANTON[2] was born on February 3, 1935 at Madrid, Boone County, Iowa. He died, age 70, of pneumonia on January 1, 2006 in the Mercy San Juan Hospital at Sacramento, California. His father was Theodore Joseph[1] Battani of Riccovolto-LaCroce, Modena Province, Italy. His mother was Anna Mary[1] Mataya [originally found as Mattheia] of the District of Tuk, Croatia, Yugoslavia.

CHARLES ANTON[2] married Kathryn Aileen "Kay" Bennett [also known as "Kathy"] in November 1966 at San Francisco [city of], California. Kathryn was born on February 12, 1944 in the San Francis Hospital at San Francisco [city of], California. Her father

Kathryn Aileen Bennett

was Tilford Oliver Monroe "Tom" Bennett of Kentucky [possibly Monroe County]. Her mother was Hazel E. Beaver [afa Bever] of Iowa and later Olympia, Thurston County, Washington [Editor's Note: On the 1840 U. S. Census for Kentucky, "Tom" and Hazel both claim to have been born in Louisiana].

Tom Bennett

"Tom" Bennett, according to family stories, was believed to be of American Indian descent [Editor's Note: His facial structure and high cheek bones might lead one to believe this to be true; however, his death certificate says he was of Irish descent]. He was born on March 23, 1898 in Kentucky. He died, age 80, of a heart attack on June 12, 1978 in the Community Memorial Hospital at Sacramento, Sacramento County, California and was cremated on June 16, 1978 and the ashes interred in the Camellia Memorial Lawn Cemetery. His father was Al Bennett of Kentucky. His mother was Aileen O'Grady of Kentucky. "Tom" was a plumber and belonged to Plumbers' Union 38.

Tom and Hazel {Beaver} Bennett

Hazel E. Beaver, according to family stories, was left at birth on the steps of a local church, supposedly by the sister of the man (Unknown) who fathered her. She was born on March 4, 1909 at Grant, Story County, Iowa. She died on November 29, 1998 at Rio Linda, Sacramento County, California. Her adopted father was Alva Edison Bennett of Illinois and later of Grant, Story County, Iowa. The name of her mother is not known.

Kathryn Bennet had married, first, Joseph R. Grindstaff on September 6, 1962 at Los Angeles, Los Angeles County, California. They were later divorced [at least by 1966 when she remarried]. He was born circa 1942. His date and place of death is not known. The name of his father and mother is not known. Kathryn and Joseph had one child:

1. Lorna Jean Grindstaff
   born on May 8, 1963 at San Francisco, California. She married Mark Dale Bender on June 26, 1982 in Martin County, Florida. Mark was born on January 28, 1962 at Washington, D.C. His father was Mark S. Bender of Washington, D.C. His mother was Sandra Barton of Kitzmiller, Gerrett County, Maryland. Lorna and Mark had six children: Dale Lee [July 4, 1984-April 14, 1996, who died at age 12 of leukemia], Hannah [born August 17, 1986, who married James Areo on February 14, 2007; later divorced], Mark Dale, Jr. [born January 17, 1991], Thomas Allen [born January 3, 1995], Kathryn

Elizabeth Sandra "Kes" [born August 1, 1997] and Ray Glenn [born April 8, 2001].

Joseph married, second, Diane G. Silva on November 26, 1983 at Solana, San Diego County, California. Diane was born circa 1942.

CHARLES ANTON[2] "Chuck" Battani moved with his parents to San Diego, San Diego County, California when he was four years old. He was educated through the public school system there until his high school years, when he attended Saint Augustine's Catholic School for Boys. While there, he learned to play the trombone and joined the high school band.

CHARLES ANTON[2] joined the United States Air Force where he continued to play the trombone in the Air Force band while also maintaining his duties as an AP — Air Policeman. He served during the Korean War. After fulfilling his four years of duty, he left the Air Force.

CHARLES ANTON[2] then went to work for General Dynamics in San Diego and entered San Diego State College where he received his Associates Degree in Radio and Television Broadcasting. While residing in San Diego, he joined the San Diego Police Reserve Unit. In 1964 he moved to San Francisco, California where he held a variety of positions, none of which challenged him or fulfilled his career goals.

CHARLES ANTON[2] married Kathryn Aileen "Kay" Bennett in November 1966 and, shortly thereafter, he secured a position assembling airplane parts with the Lockheed Company. When the company offered an opportunity to further his education and become a computer software engineer, he quickly signed up. He was transferred to the Lockheed Space Program at San Jose, Santa Clara, California, where he and Kay bought their first house. Two years later he was transferred to Lockheed's facility at NASA [the National Aeronautics and Space Administration] at Houston [city of], Texas. While there, he was involved in writing the software programs for the Lunar Landing Module Trainer in preparation for the first Lunar Landing on the Moon. Shortly after the first Lunar Landing he was transferred back to San Jose, California. With budget cuts instituted by then President Richard M. Nixon, "Chuck" was laid off from Lockheed.

CHARLES ANTON[2] quickly found work at Dalmo Victor, a San Jose defense contracting company. While with Dalmo Victor, he was sent to Israel for seven months to aid the Israeli Air Force with software development for their military aircraft. Upon re-turning to the United States, he found that he required new challenges and moved to a new position on the East Coast.

CHARLES ANTON[2] secured a position as a software programmer with Ford Aerospace in Baltimore, Maryland. However, the commute from Sterling Park, Loudoun County, Virginia became a burden and he secured a new position with E-Systems at Reston, Fairfax County, Virginia. When he lost his job with E-Systems, he and Kay decided to move back to California.

CHARLES ANTON[2] and Kay moved to Rio Linda, Sacramento County, California in October 1991 where they last resided at 6836 4th Avenue. After moving there they assisted in the care of Kay's parents, who were in very poor health. "Chuck" took a job as a security guard and worked in that capacity until he retired, at age 69. After his death, Kay sold their home and moved to the Weeksville area of Pasquotank County, North Carolina. In 2010 she moved to Port St. Lucie, St. Lucie County, Florida [where in 2015 she currently resides] to be near her other daughter Lorna and her family.

The Children of
Charles Anton[2] Battani
and Kathryn Aileen "Kay" Bennett

1 **Elizabeth Ann[3] Battani**
born on August 31, 1972 at 2:33 pm, 5lbs, 10½
ounces in the Alexian Brothers Hospital at San
Jose, Santa Clara County, California. Elizabeth[3]
married, first, Ronald Hilton[8] Dovel of Stephens
City, Frederick County, Virginia. Ronald[8] was born
on June 30, 1964 at Winchester, Frederick County,
Virginia. Elizabeth Ann[3] and Ronald[8] were di-
vorced on April 24, 1998 at Winchester, Frederick
County, Virginia. His father was Richard Harvey[7]
[Carl Sylvester[6] {of Stanley, Page County, Vir-
ginia}, William Tazewell[5] {of East Liberty, Page
County, Virginia}, Peter Simon[4], William[3] {of
Alma, Rockingham County, Virginia}, David S.[2],
Jr., David S.[1] {of England and later of Ingham,
Rockingham County, Virginia}] Dovel. His mother
was Wanda Jean[8] [Roy Cecil Riley[7], William
Fulton[6] {of Indian Creek, Tazwell County, Vir-
ginia}, Riley A.[5] {of Harmon, Tazwell County,
Virginia}, William A.[4] {of Montgomery County,
Virginia}, David Riley[3], Emera[2] {of Dutchess
County, New York}, Johan Peter[1] {Althauser of
Segendorff, Germany}, Wilmhelm[1a], Jacob[2a]]
Altizer of Tazwell County, Virginia. Elizabeth[3] and
Ronald[8] had two children: Dakota Orion[9] and

Jacob Michael[9].

Elizabeth[3] married, second, Christopher Philip[11] Colson on September 16, 1997 at Statesville, Iredell County, North Carolina. Elizabeth[3] and Christopher[11] were divorced on June 30, 2005 in Pasquotank County, North Carolina. He was born on July 6, 1970 in the Calambrone Military Hospital at Pisa, Tuscany, Italy. His biological father was Philip Alan[5] [Leo Francis[4], Oscar Joseph[3], Ernest Albert[2], William[1] {of England}, (Mary[1a] or Sarah[1a]), George[2a], Friend[3a]] Coleman of Landover, Prince Georges County, Maryland. His adoptive father was Stanton Darnbrook[10] [Douglas Herman[9], Henry Wilson[8], Stanton E(phraim)[7], Theophilus T.[6] 2nd, Ephraim[5], Ichabod Downs[4], Hatevil[3], Samuel[2], Cornelius[1], Jan Cornelissen[1a] Van Rotterdam {of Rotterdam, The Netherlands}, Cornelius Jonckers[2a]] Colson of Cambridge, Middlesex County, Massachusetts. His mother was Donna Marie[5] [Robert Charles[4] Joseph Francis[3], John Joseeph[2], John[1] {of Ireland}] Higgins of Washington, D. C. Elizabeth[3] and Christopher[11] had two children: Quinn Higgins[12] and Charles Darnbrook[12].

ELIZABETH ANN[3] married, third, Wolfgang[1] Murlebach on October 18, 2014 at Port St. Lucie, St. Lucie County, Florida in the office of the

County Clerk of the Circuit Court Annex. Wolfgang[1] was born on March 9, 1966 in Germany. The name of his father and mother is not known.

Wolfgang[1] had married, first, Maria Nella Ortiz. Their divorce was recorded on March 15, 2010 at Stuart, Stuart County, Florida.

The Wedding of
Theodore Joseph[1] Battani and Anna Mary[2] Mataya
Front Row: Jeana Battani, (Unid) Little Girl, (Unid) Man,
Theodore Joseph Battani and (Unid) Little Boy; Middle
Row: Anna Mary Mataya; Back Row: Penechie Battani
Mataya, (Unid) Man, Julia Mataya, (Unid) Man, (Unid)
Woman, Frank Mataya and Vance Mataya

Life and Times of
Theodore Joseph[1] Battani

PATERNAL ANCESTRY: [BATTANI: Camillo[1a] "Charles," Ricardo[2a], Luigi[3a]]

MATERNAL ANCESTRY: [STEFANI: Olivia Victoria[1a] "Eva," Giovanni[2a]]

THEODORE JOSEPH[1] [Editor's Note: Another record shows him [incorrectly] as Theodore Daniel] was born on July 4, 1905 at Riccovolto-LaCroce, Modena Province, Italy. He died, age 58, of heart failure on September 5, 1963 in his home at 6831 Savage Court, San Diego, San Diego County, California and was buried there on September 10, 1963 in the Holy Cross Cemetery. His father was Camillo[1a] "Charles" Battani of Modena Province, Italy. His mother was Olivia Victoria[1a] "Eva" Stefani of Italy.

THEODORE JOSEPH[1] "Tito" married Anna Mary[2] Mataya originally found as

Anna Mataya and Theodore Joseph Battani Wedding

Mattheia] on September 6, 1930 in St. Malachy's Catholic Church at Madrid, Boone County, Iowa. Officiating was the Reverend Newman Flanagan. Vance[2] Mataya and Penechie[2] Battani were witnesses. Anna[2] was born on March 22, 1907 at Hancock, Houghton County, Michigan and was baptized there on March 31, 1907 by the Reverend T. J. Atfield at St. Patrick's Catholic Church. She died on October 20, 1992 at San Diego, San Diego County, California. Her father was Anton[1] "Tony" [also known as "Anthony"] Mataya [originally found as Mattheia] of the District of Tuk, Croatia, Yugoslavia and later of Trimountain, Houghton County, Michigan. Her mother was Antonia[1] Kruzich of Yugoslavia and later of Trimountain, Houghton County, Michigan.

Antoni "Tony" Mataya and Antonia {Kruzich} Mataya

Anton[1] "Tony" Mataya was born on June 10, 1878 in Croatia and died on May 20, 1958 in San Diego, San Diego County, California. He, age 27, married Antonia[1] Kruzich, age 24, on July 15, 1905 by F. Richter [a Catholic priest] at Atlantic,

Houghton County, Michigan. His father was Simon[1a] "Sam" Mataya of the District of Tuk, Croatia, Yugoslavia. His mother was Margaret[1a] Yurkovich of Croatia.

Antonia[1] Kruzich was born on December 20, 1880 in Yugoslavia. She, a resident of 3602 S. Cordova, Spring Valley, San Diego County, California, died, age 73, of heart failure at 8:00 am on November 23, 1954 at the San Diego Edgemoor County Farm at Santee, San Diego County, California. Her father was Peter[1a] Kruzich of Yugoslavia. Her mother was Helen[1a] Juracovic of Yugoslavia. Her Certificate of Naturalization #7029452, Petition #16671, dated July 11, 1952 notes her as married and residing at 7628 Westmoreland Street, San Diego, California.

THEODORE JOSEPH[2] lived in Woodward, Dallas County, Iowa before he moved to San Diego, San Diego County, California where for the last seventeen years of his life he worked as a truck driver for San Diego Forwarding Company.

The Children of
Theodore Joseph[1] Battani
and Anna Mary[2] Mataya

1. **Cathryne Sylvia[2] Battani**
   born on November 8, 1933 at Madrid, Boone
   County, Iowa and was baptized there according to
   the Rite of the Roman Catholic Church by the
   Reverend John F. Cain on December 3, 1933 in St.
   Malachy's Catholic Church. Her sponsors were
   Vance[2] Mataya and his wife, Penechie[2] Battani
   Mataya. Cathryne[2] died, age about 4 months, in
   March 1934 at Madrid, Boone County, Iowa.

2. **Charles Anton[2] Battani**
   born on February 3, 1935 at Madrid, Boone
   County, Iowa. He died on January 1, 2006 at Rio
   Linda, Sacramento County, California. He married
   Kathryn Aileen "Kay" Bennett [also known as
   "Kathy"] in November 1966 at San Francisco [city
   of], California. Kathryn was born on February 12,
   1944 in the San Francis Hospital at San Francisco,
   California. Her father was Tilford Oliver Monroe
   "Tom" [Al] Bennett of Kentucky [possibly Monroe
   County]. Her mother was Hazel Beaver [some-
   times found as Bever] of Iowa and later Olympia,
   Washington. Charles[2] and Kathryn had one child:
   Elizabeth Ann[3].

Camillo Battani

The Life and Times of
Camillo[1a] "Charles" Battani

PATERNAL ANCESTRY: [BATTANI: Ricardo[2a], Luigi[3a]]

MATERNAL ANCESTRY: [STEFANI: Carola]

CAMILLO[1a] was born on March 29, 1874 at Rampada, Italy. He died of spinal meningitis in 1936 at Des Moines, Pok County, Iowa. His father was Ricardo[2a] Battani of Italy. His mother was Carola Stefani of Italy.

[EDITOR'S NOTE: A descendant in Italy says that the family was from Appennino, Tosco, Emiliano, Italy;

an American descendant says they were from Riccovolto-LaCroce, Modena Province, Italy]

CAMILLO[1a] married Oliva Victoria[1] "Eva" Stefani of Italy sometime before 1903 [when their first child was born] in Modena Province, Italy. Oliva[1] was born on March 22, 1881 at Riccovolto, Modena, Italy. She died on April 21, 1964 at Granger, Dallas County, Iowa and was buried in

Camillo "Charles" Battani and Oliva Victoria "Eva" Stefani

the Beaver Catholic Cemetery. Her father was Luigi[1a] [Giovanni[2a]] Stefani of Frassinoro, Modena, Emilia-Romagne, Italy. Her mother was Carolina[1a] [Vincenzo[2a] {of Gallicano, Lucca, Toscana, Italy}] Fiori of Frassinoro, Modena, Emilia-Romagne, Italy.

CAMILLO[1a] "Charles" and his family emigrated from Italy, departing from Genoa aboard the ship *Conte Di Savoia*, arriving in New York City, New York on September 7, 1935.

CAMILLO[1a] is found on the 1920 U. S. Census at Woodward, Dallas County, Iowa, age 45, a coal miner, with his wife, Eva, age 38, Richard, age 16, Tito, age 14, James, age 12, Dante, age 10, Alpenice, age 8, Bruno, age 6, Sesto, age $4^{11/12ths}$, Erma, age $2^{10/12ths}$ and Aldo, age $^{11/12ths}$.

Camillo Battani Family
BR L/R–Sasto, Bruno,
Dante, James, Theodore
& Ricco
FR L/R–Erma, Camillo,
Aldo, Ray, Oliva &
Penechie

The Children of
Camillo[1a] "Charles" Battani
and Oliva Victoria[1] "Eva" Stefani

1. Ricco J.[1] "Richard" Battani
   born on May 4, 1903 at Riccovolto-LaCroce,
   Modena Province, Italy. He died in April 1978 at
   Granger, Dallas County, Iowa. He married Amelia
   M.[2] Danti. Their date of marriage, probably in
   Dallas County, Iowa, is not known. Amelia[2] was
   born on March 25, 1907 at Bevier, Macon County,
   Missouri. She died on January 30, 1975 at Granger,
   Dallas County, Iowa. Her father was James[1] Danti
   of Italy and later of Missouri. Her mother was
   Irene (Unknown) of Italy and later of Missouri.

Ricco[1] and Amelia[2] had one child: name not known.

2. **Theodore Joseph[1] "Tito" Battani**
   [Editor's Note: Another researcher calls him, incorrectly, Theodore David Battani] born on July 4, 1905 at Riccovolto-LaCroce, Modena Province, Italy. He died, age 58, of heart failure on September 5, 1963 in his home at 6831 Savage Court, San Diego, San Diego County, California and was buried there on September 10, 1963 in the Holy Cross Cemetery. He married Anna Mary[2] Mataya [originally found as Mattheia] on September 6, 1930 in St. Malachy's Catholic Church at Madrid, Boone County, Iowa, the Reverend Newman Flanagan officiating. Vance[2] Mataya and Penechie[1] Battani were witnesses. Anna[2] was born on March 22, 1907 at Hancock, Houghton County, Michigan and was baptized there on March 31, 1907 by the Reverend T. J. Atfield at St. Patrick's Catholic Church. She died on October 20, 1992 at San Diego, San Diego County, California. Her father was Anton[1] "Tony" [also known as "Anthony"] Mataya [originally found as Mattheia] of the District of Tuk, Croatia, Yugoslavia and later of Trimountain, Houghton County, Michigan. Her mother was Antonia[1] Kruzich of Yugoslavia and later of Trimountain, Houghton County, Michigan. Theodore[1] and

Anna[2] had two children: Cathayna Sylvia[2] and Charles Anton[2].

3. **James Benedict[1] "Jim" Battani**
born on November 3, 1907 at Riccovolto-LaCroce, Modena Province, Italy. He died in May 1987 at Woodward, Dallas County, Iowa. He married Gena M.[2] Logli sometime before 1933 [when their first child was born], probably in Dallas County, Iowa. She was born on July 27, 1908 at Riolunato, Italy. She died in May 1995 at Woodward, Dallas County, Iowa. Her father was Valentino[1] "Voley" Logli of Riolunato, Italy. Her mother was Chiara[1] "Clara" Zagnoli of Riolunato, Italy. Gena[2] arrived in America with her mother on December 11, 1910 on the ship *La Lorraine* from Le Havre, France to New York [Editor's Note: They were coming to join Valentino[1], who was already in Des Moines, Des Moines County, Iowa; he arrived on January 13, 1901 from Le Havre, France to New York on the ship *La Champagne*]. James[1] and Gena[2] lived at Woodward, Dallas County, Iowa. James[1] and Gena[2] had two children:

a. **James Lee[2] "Jim" Battani**
born on January 31, 1933 at Woodward, Dallas County, Iowa. He died, age 79, of a heart ailment on February 24, 1995 at Woodward, Dallas County, Iowa and was buried there in

35

the Woodward Cemetery. He married Mary Ellen^9 Whitfield on June 30, 1953 at Fulton, Itawamba County, Mississippi. She was born circa 1932 in Franklin County, Alabama. Her date and place of death is not known. Her father was Jimmy Chester^8 [Macky Donald^7 "Mack," William C.^{6} {of Edgecomb County, North Carolina}, Benjamin^5, Benjamin^4 {of Martin County, North Carolina}, Joel I.^{3}, William Joseph^2 {of Beaufort County, South Carolina}, Thomas^1 {of Hexham, Northumberland, England}, John^{1a} {of Haydon Bridge, England}] Whitfield of Tishomingo County, Mississippi. Her mother was Carson Willie^8 [John Thomas^7, Jeremiah Dailey^6, William Hightower^5, Charnel Hightower^4 {"M.D." of Kershaw District, South Carolina}, Presley^3 {of North Carolina}, Merryman Joseph^2 {of Richmond County, Virginia}, Thomas^1 {of England}] Thorn of Old Burlington, Franklin County, Alabama. James^2 and Mary^9 had two children: James Lee^3 "Jimmy" and Gina Marie^3.

b. Dale Landi^2 Battani
born circa 1937 at Woodward, Dallas County, Iowa. Her date and place of death is not known.

4. Dante Alfredo^1 "Don" Battani
born on March 8, 1909 at Woodward, Dallas

County, Iowa. He died on April 12, 1972 at Granger, Dallas County, Iowa and was buried there in the Beaver Catholic Cemetery. He married Esther[3] Rosetta September 23, 1933 at Madrid, Boone County, Iowa. She was born on June 10, 1916 at Centerville, Appanoose County, Iowa. She died on March 26, 2008 at Granger, Dallas County, Iowa and was buried there in the Beaver Catholic Cemetery. Her father was John Baptist[2] [Joseph[1] {of Brovengo, Italy}] Rosetta of Osage City, Osage County, Kansas. Her mother was Lucinda[2] "Lucy" [Tony[1] {of Italy}] Delaponte of Osage County, Kansas. Dante[1] and Esther[3] had two children:

a. Edward G.[2] Battani
   born in 1944 at Granger, Dallas County, Iowa. He died, age 21, in 1965 at Granger, Dallas County, Iowa.

b. Mary Ellen[2] Battani
   born circa 1909 at Granger, Dallas County, Iowa. Her date and place of death is not known. She married Fred J. McKibbin. Mary[2] and Fred had two children: Edward and Elizabeth.

Esther[3] married, second, Elio A.[2] Biondi in 1979, presumably at Granger, Dallas County, Iowa. He was born on March 31, 1911 at Granger, Dallas County, Iowa. He died on September 8, 1997 at

Granger, Dallas County, Iowa and was buried there in the Beaver Catholic Cemetery. His father was Giuseppi[1] "Joseph" [Pasquale Dominico[1a]] Biondi of Italy and later of Granger, Dallas County, Iowa. His mother was Mary Berti[1] [Vencenzo[1a]] (Unknown) of Italy. There was no issue.

5. Alpenice Marie[1] "Penechie" Battani
   born on January 15, 1912 at Carney, Polk County, Iowa [another record says Woodward, Dallas County, Iowa]. She died on September 2, 1996 at Madrid, Boone County, Iowa. She married Vinces[2] Las Anton "Vance" Mataya. Their date and place of marriage is not known. Vance[2] was born on April 21, 1906 at Quincy, Branch County, Michigan. He died on December 3, 1989 in Boone County, Iowa. His father was Anton[1] "Tony" {afa Anthony} Mataya of the District of Tuk, Croatia, Yugoslavia. His mother was Antonja[1] "Antonia" [Peter[1a]] Kruzich of Yugoslavia. Penechie[1] and Vance[2] resided in Madrid, Boone County, Iowa. Penechie[1] and Vance[2] had five children:

   a. Joseph[3] Mataya
      born circa 1932 at Madrid, Boone County, Iowa. His date and place of death is not known.

   b. Caroline[3] Mataya
      born circa 1935 at Madrid, Boone County, Iowa.

Her date and place of death is not known.

c. Dolores[3] Mataya
    born circa 1936 at Madrid, Boone County, Iowa.
    Her date and place of death is not known.

d. Henry[3] "Louie" Mataya
    date of birth at Madrid, Boone County, Iowa is
    not known. His date and place of death is not
    known.

e. John[3] "Johnnie" Mataya
    date of birth at Madrid, Boone County, Iowa is
    not known. His date and place of death is not
    known.

6. Bruno Carlo[1] Battani
    born on October 22, 1913 at Riccovolto-LaCroce,
    Modena Province, Italy. He died on June 11, 2000
    at Woodward, Dallas County, Iowa and was
    buried there in the Beaver Catholic Cemetery at
    Granger, Dallas County, Iowa. He married Geneva
    M. (Unknown). The date and place of their
    marriage is not known. She was born on May 6,
    1919 at Lexington, LaFayette County, Missouri.
    She died, age 76, of heart failure on August 18,
    1995 at Granger Manor, Dallas County, Iowa and
    was buried there in the Beaver Catholic Cemetery
    at Granger, Dallas County, Iowa. He lived at

Woodward, Dallas County, Iowa. Bruno[1] and Geneva had four children: (son)[2], Robert D.[2] [born circa 1939], Ron[2] and Lee[2].

7. Sasto Dorando[1] Battani
born on February 14, 1915 at Woodward, Dallas County [another researcher says Carney, Polk County], Iowa. He died on December 27, 1976 at Des Moines, Polk County, Iowa and was buried there on December 30, 1976 in the Glendale Cemetery. He married Margaret Jane Foster sometime before 1934 [when their first child was born] in Dallas County, Iowa. She was born on February 2, 1916 in Dallas County, Iowa. She died on May 7, 1958 at Des Moines, Boone County, Iowa. Her father was Oren A. Foster of Dallas County, Iowa. Her mother was Jessie E. Fleming of Polk County, Iowa. Sasto[1] completed two years of high school, was a private in the U. S. Army and later became a retail manager. Sasto[1] and Margaret had five children:

a. Eugene R.[2] "Gene" Battani
born circa 1933 either at Des Moines, Des Moines County, Iowa. He died on January 31, 2014 in the Iowa Methodist Medical Center at Des Moines, Des Moines County, Iowa and was cremated and the ashes interred in the Iowa Veterans Cemetery at Adel. He married Louise

Hovy at Omaha, Douglas County, Nebraska. Eugene[2] and Louise had a child: Kristina Marie[3].

b. Cherrie[2] Battani
   born circa 1938 at Des Moines, Des Moines County, Iowa. Her date and place of death is not known. She married Leon Praeuner.

c. Terry[2] Battani
   born at Des Moines, Des Moines County, Iowa, is not known. His date and place of death is not known. He married Sandy (Unknown).

d. Lawrenna Foster[2] "Larry" Battani
   born at Des Moines, Des Moines County, Iowa, is not known. His date and place of death is not known.

e. Pamela[2] "Pam" Battani
   date of birth at Des Moines, Des Moines County Iowa is not known. Her date and place of death is not known. She married (Unknown) Monroe.

8. Irma M.[1] Battani
   born circa March 1917 at Woodward, Dallas County, Iowa. She died in April 1983 at Mountain Home, Baxter County, Arkansas. She married Harold George Kinney on April 18, 1970 in Polk

County, Iowa. He was born on December 31, 1911 at Bedford, Taylor County, Iowa. He died in April 1983 at Mountain Home, Baxter County, Arkansas. His father was Thomas Valentine "Tine" [George B. {of Derby Township, Union County, Ohio}, William] Kinney of Plattesville, Taylor County, Iowa. His mother was Ida Myrtle[9] [William Harrison[8] "Will" {of Jay, Franklin County, Maine}, Sumner[7], James[6] {of Gilmenton, Belknap County, New Hampshire}, Joshua[5] {of Exeter, Rockingham County, New Hampshire}, Joshua[4], John[3], James[2], John[1] {of Scotland}] Bean of New Market, Taylor County, Iowa. There was no issue.

Harold had married, first, Eleanor Ann[3] "Ellie" Barton on April 9, 1935 in Iowa. She was born on September 23, 1914 in Iowa. She died on December 22, 2007 in Polk County, Iowa. Her father was Christian August[2] "Christ" [Christian Henirich[1] {of Rosenhagen, Mecklenburg-Streitzi, Germany}, Carl Heinrich Christian[1a] {of Langendorf, Aachen, Nordhein-Westfalen, Germany}, Johannes Joachim[2a] {of Muisall, Gustrow, Mechlinburg-Vorpommern, Germany}] Barton of Jackson, Jackson County, Iowa. Her mother was Emma Barbara[2] [Frederick[1] "Fred" {of Germany}, Frederick[1a]] Ross of Lincoln, Audubon County, Iowa. Harold and Eleanor[3] had four children: Marlene Barbara, Harold George, Barton Thomas and Sue Ann.

9. Aldo[1] Battani
born on January 31, 1919 in Polk County, Iowa. He died, age 17, on March 31, 1936 in Dallas County, Iowa and was buried there at Granger.

10. Raymond Robert[1] "Ray" Battani
born on May 29, 1924 at Woodward, Dallas County, Iowa. He died on March 22, 1998 [another record says 1991] at Ankeny, Polk County, Iowa. He married Mary E. Stone. The date and place of their marriage is not known. She was born on November 12, 1925, probably in Dallas County, Iowa. She died, age 75, on May 23, 2001 at Ankeny, Polk County, Iowa and was buried there in Highland Memorial Gardens. Her father was Kenneth Porter [Porter O. {of Vermont}, Ovette E.] Stone of Prophetstown, Whiteside County, Illinois and later of Beaver, Dallas County, Iowa. Her mother was Nellie Mae[4] [William Henry[3], Louis N.[2] {of Plattsburgh, Clinton County, New York}, Charles[1] {afa Menard of Canada}, Paschel[1a] {of Quebec, Provence of Quebec, Canada}, Pashel[2a], Jean Baptiste[3a], Jean Baptiste[4a], Louis[5a] {known as Menard Fontaine}, Jacques[6a] {born circa 1628}] Miner of Anamesa, Jones County, Iowa. Ray[1] and Mary had three children: two sons and one daughter (names unknown).

The Life and Times of
Ricardo[2a] Battani

PATERNAL ANCESTRY: [BATTANI: Luigi[3a] {of Riccovolto, de Modena, Italy}]

MATERNAL ANCESTRY: [BALDUCCHI: Maria Santa {of Riccovolto, de Modena, Italy}]

RICARDO[2a] was born on January 24, 1847 at Rampada [some say Riccovolto] de Modena, Italy. His date and place of death is not known. His father was Luigi[3a] Battani of Riccovolto, de Modena, Italy. His mother was Maria Santa Balducchi of Riccovolto, de Modena, Italy.

RICARDO[2a] married Carola [afa Carolina] Stefani of Italy sometime before 1869 [when their first child was born] in Modena Provence, Italy. Carola was born on January 16, 1850 at Riccovolto-La Crocein de Modena, Italy. She died in 1928 in Italy. The name of her father and mother is not known.

RICARDO[2a] was purported to have helped build the bell tower at Riccovolto, de Modena, Italy.

The Children of
Ricardo[2a] Battani
and Carola Stefani

1. **Biagio[1a] Battani**
born on April 13, 1869 at Ricovolto-La Crocein de Modena, Italy. He died in 1961 in Italy. He married, first, Camilla (Unknown). Biagio[1a] was blind. Biagio[1a] and Camilla had three children: Lidwa[1], Pietro[1] and Leardo[1].

   Biagio[1a] married, second, Camilla's sister, Lucia (Unknown). Biagio[1a] and Lucia had two children: Riccardo[1] and Maria[1].

2. **Camillo[1a] "Charles" Battani**
born on March 29, 1874 at Riccovolto-La Crocein de Modena, Italy. He died of spinal meningitis on May 12, 1936 in Dallas County, Iowa and was buried there in the Beaver Catholic Cemetery at Granger, Dallas County, Iowa. He married Oliva Victoria[1] "Eva" Stefani, sometime before 1903 [when their first child was born] in Riccovolto, Italy. Oliva[1] was born on March 22, 1881 in Italy. She died in April 1964 in Dallas County, Iowa and was buried there in the Beaver Catholic Cemetery at Granger, Dallas County, Iowa. Her father was Luigi[1a] [Giovanni[2a]] Stefani of Frassinoro, Modena, Emilia-Romagne, Italy. Her mother was Carolina[1a]

[Vincenzo[2a] {of Gallicano, Lucca, Toscana, Italy}] Fiori of Frassinoro, Modena, Emilia-Romagne, Italy. Camillo[1a] and Oliva[1] had ten children: Ricco J.[1] "Richard", Theodore Joseph[1] "Tito," James Benedict[1] "Jim," Dante Alfredo[1] "Don," Alpenice Marie[1] "Penechie," Bruno Carlo[1], Sasto Dorando[1], Irma M.[1], Aldo[1] and Raymond Robert[1] "Ray."

3. Luigi[1a] Battani

   born on July 5, 1876 at Riccovolto-La Crocein de Modena, Italy. He died in 1925 in Italy. He married Angela (Unknown). Luigi[1a] and Angela had three children: Guiliano[1], Elena[1] and Alma[1].

4. Marco[1a] Battani

   born on January 9, 1882 at Riccovolto-La Crocein de Modena, Italy. He died, age 103, in 1985 at La Croce, Frassinoro, Modena, Italy. He married Maria Nicolini in 1909 at Riccovolto, Modena, Italy. Her date and place of birth is not known. Before he married Maria, on June 30, 1906 he had sailed from Le Havre, France aboard the French ship *La Touraine*, arriving in New York on July 8, 1906. Apparantly, he returned for his marriage. He and his family lived in the house where his sister Gelsumina[1a] was born at La Croce, Modena Province, Italy. After his wife died, he lived with his daughter Elia[1] until he died. Marco[1a] and Maria had six children:

a. Nello[1] Battani
born on November 11, 1911 at La Croce, Frassinoro, Modena, Italy. He died on January 2, 1982 at Des Moines, Polk County, Iowa. He married Sofia G.[2] "Beba" Milani. She was born on July 2, 1912 at Cambira, Weston County, Wyoming. She died on September 23, 2014 at Madrid, Boone County, Iowa. Her father was Enrico[1] Milani of Cargedolo, Modena, Italy. Her mother was Amabile Clotilde[1] (Unknown} of Modena, Italy and later of Madrid, Boone County, Iowa. Nello[1] and his family departed Genoa, Italy, arriving on March 19, 1950 in New York City, New York aboard the ship *Conte Bianamano*. Nello[1] and Sofia[2] had three children: Mariano[2], Lorenzo[2] and Juliane[2].

b. Alberto[1] "Berto" Battani
born circa 1914 in Modena, Italy. He died in 2004 in Modena, Italy.

c. Elia[1] Battani
born circa 1916/1917 in Modena, Italy. His date and place of birth is not known.

d. Lonino[1] Battani
born circa 1918/1919 in Modena, Italy. His date and place of birth is not known.

e. Allimano[1] Battani
born circa 1922 in Modena, Italy. He died in 1942 in Modena, Italy.

f. Antonio[1] Battani
born circa 1936 in Modena, Italy. He died in 2003 in Modena, Italy.

5. Rocco[1a] Battani
born on August 22, 1885 at Riccovolto-La Crocein de Modena, Italy. He died in April 1968 at Granger, Dallas County, Iowa and was buried there in the Beaver Catholic Cemetery. He married Camilla[1] [afa Cillini] Fontanini in Italy. Camilla was born on April 19, 1886 in Italy. She died on June 18, 1946 in Dallas County, Iowa and was buried there in the Beaver Catholic Cemetery. Her father was Theodore[1a] Fontanini of Italy. Her mother was Domenica[1a] (Unknown) of Italy. They immigrated to the U. S. in 1910. In 1930 they were living in Detroit, Wayne County, Michigan. Rocco[1a] and Camilla[1] had six children:

a. Anita Marie[1] Battani
born on April 16, 1911 at Des Moines, Polk County, Iowa. She died in August 1990 in Des Moines, Polk County, Iowa. She married Ricardo Victor[2] "Richard" Vignaroli on July 25, 1931 at Des Moines, Polk County. He was born

on May 21, 1909 at Colfax, Jasper County, Iowa. He died on May 4, 1984 at Des Moines, Polk County, Iowa. His father was Lorenzo[1] [Antoinio[1a]] Vignaroli of Frassingoro, Modena, Eimilia, Romagan, Italy. His mother was Genoveffa[1] "Jennie" [Ferdinando[1a]] Banneti [afa Romitti] of Frassinoro, Modena, Eimilia, Romagan, Italy. Ricardo[2] enlisted in the U. S. Army as a private on April 22, 1944 at Camp Dodge, Johnston, Herrald County, Iowa. He was discharged in November 1945. He only had three years of high school but made a good living as an electrician. Anita[1] and Ricardo[2] had three children: names not known.

b. Frank[1] Battani
born in 1912 at Des Moines, Polk County, Iowa. He died in 1937. His place of death is not known.

c. Mary[1] "Norma" Battani
born in 1914 at High Bridge, Boone County, Iowa. She died in 2004 at Granger, Dallas County, Iowa.

d. Guliano[1] "Robert" Battani
born in 1915 at Des Moines, Polk County, Iowa. He died in 1987 at Ankeny, Polk County, Iowa.

e. Aldo P.[1] Battani
    born in February 1917 at High Bridge, Boone
    County, Iowa. He died, age 84, in October 2001
    an Ankeny, Polk County, Iowa and was buried
    there in Ankany Memorial Cemetery.

f. Clara[1] Battani
    date of birth, either in Des Moines, Polk County
    or High Bridge, Boone County, Iowa, is not
    known. Her date and place of death is not
    known.

6. Genoeffa[1a] Battani
    born on August 18 [another record says the 13th],
    1887 at Riccovolto-La Crocein de Modena, Italy.
    She died of heart trouble on January 21, 1963 in
    Italy. She married (Dominico?) Battani. Genoeffa[1a]
    and (Dominico) had seven children: Etore, Dante,
    Guido, Aldo, Ada, Tina and Camille.

7. Gelsumina[1a] "Josephine" Battani
    born on June 6, 1889 [another record says June 4,
    1888] at Riccovolto-La Crocein de Modena, Italy.
    She died from heart trouble in January 1959 in
    Polk County, Iowa. She married Attilio Antonia[1]
    Bianchi. Attilio[1] was born on March 15, 1884 in
    Modeno Province, Italy. He was killed by a falling
    tree on November 17, 1953 in Polk County, Iowa.
    His father was Guiseppi[1a] Bianchi of Sassostomo,

de Modena, Italy. His mother was Beatrice[1a] Ugolini of Castellino, Riolunato, de Modena, Italy. In 1940, Attilio[1] and his family were living at Saylor, Polk County, Iowa. Gelsumina[1a] and Attilio[1] had five children:

a. Ismene Beatrice[2] Bianchi
   date and place of birth, presumably in Polk County, Iowa, is not known. Her date and place of death is not known.

b. Robert[2] Bianchi
   date and place of birth, presumably in Polk County, Iowa, is not known. His date and place of death is not known.

c. Nellie Katherine[2] Bianch
   born on November 13, 1921 in Polk County, Iowa. She died on May 8, 2013 at Columbus, Franklin County, Ohio. She married James Clinton[10] Coe, Jr. Their date of marriage, presumably in Ohio, is not known. He was born on March 28, 1921 at Mt. Vernon, Knox County, Ohio. He died on December 5, 1990 at Columbus, Franklin County, Ohio. His father was James Clinton[9] [William Henry[8], James Wesley[7] {of Marshall County, West Virginia}, John[6] {of Washington County, Pennsylvania}, Isaac Newton[5], Philip[4] {of Morristown, Morris

County, New Jersey}, Benjamin^3 {of Jamaica, Queens County, New York}, Joseph^2, Benjamin^1 {of Boxford, Suffolk, England}, Robert^{1a} {of Thorpe Morieux, Suffolk, England}, Henry^{2a} {of Great Maplestead, Essex, England}, John^{3a} {Coo the Elder}, John^{4a}, John^{5a}, Thomas^{6a}, John^{7a}, John^{8a}, John^{9a} {Coo born circa 1340 of Gestingthorpe, Essex, England}] Coe of Knox County, Ohio. His mother was Jocelyn Mae^6 [Robert Calvin^5 {of Brock's Creek, Rockingham County, Virginia}, David^4, John^3 {afa Impswiller}, Jacob^2 {of York, York County, Pennsylvania}, Peter^1 {of Germany}] Emsweller of Mt. Vernon, Knox County, Ohio. Nellie^2 appears on the 1840 U. S. Census, age 18, living at home, a laundress. Nellie^2 and James^{10} had two children: (child)^{11} and James Clinton^{11} III.

d. Lena^2 Bianchi
born circa 1924 in Polk County, Iowa. Her date and place of death is not known.

e. Carolina^2 "Caroline" Bianchi
born circa 1929 in Polk County, Iowa. Her date and place of death is not known.

8. Adolpho^{1a} "Adolfo" Battani
born on March 17, 1893 [his social security death record says May 11, 1893] at Riccovolto-La Crocein

de Modena, Italy. He died, age 78, on September 2, 1971 at Madrid, Boone County, Iowa and was buried there in Mount Hope Cemetery. He married Pia Battani. The date of their marriage, presumable in Riccovolto, Italy, is not known. She was born in 1896 in Riccovolto, Italy. She died in 1940 at Madrid, Boone County, Iowa and was buried there in Mount Hope Cemetery. Her father was Angelo Battani of Fontanolucia, Italy. The name of her mother is not known. Adolpho[1a] left the port of LeHavre, France on the ship *Melita* and arrived at St. John, New Brunswick, Canada, then crossed the border into the United States on December 6, 1920. He was a coal miner. Adolpho[1a] and Pia had three children:

a. Lena Marie[1] Battani
   born on October 29, 1920 in Modena, Italy. She died on June 18, 2015 at Gladstone, Clay County, Missouri. She married Ray Girton on August 1, 1942 at Madrid, Boone County, Iowa. Lena[1] and Ray had two children: Nancy and Brenda.

b. Luigi[1] "George" Battani
   born on August 1, 1922 in Boone County, Iowa. He died in August 1978 at Madrid, Boon County, Iowa. He married Darlene M. (Unknown). She was born in 1929 [per tombstone].

She died in 1962 [per tombstone].

c. Gino[1] Battani
born on December 25, 1929 in Boone County,
Iowa. He died on June 18, 1953 at Madrid,
Boone County, Iowa.

9. Brigida[1a] Battani
born on July 16, 1895 at Riccovolto-La Crocein de
Modena, Italy. She died circa 1983/1984, presumably in Argentina. She married Ernesto Fiori
and removed to Argentina. Brigida[1a] and Ernesto
had two children: Lade and Mari.

The Life and Times of
Luigi[3a] Battani

PATERNAL ANCESTRY: [BATTANI: (Unknown)]

MATERNAL ANCESTRY: [(UNKNOWN)]

LUIGI[3a] was born circa 1835 at Riccovolto de Modena, Italy. His date of death in Italy is not known. The name of his father and mother is not known.

LUIGI[3a] married Maria Santa Balducchi of Riccovolto de Modena, Italy. The date and place of their marriage is not known. Maria was born circa 1839 in Italy. Her date of death in Italy is not known. The name of her father and mother is not known.

The Children of
Luigi[3a] Battani
and Maria Santa Balducchi

1. **Ricardo[2a] Battani**
   born in 1847 at Riccovolto-La Crocein de Modena, Italy. His date and place of death is not known. He married Carola Stefani of Italy sometime before 1869 [when their first child was born]. Carola was born on January 16, 1850 at Riccovolto-La Crocein de Modena, Italy. She died in 1928 in Italy. The name of her father and mother is not known.

Ricardo[2a] and Carola had nine children: Biagio[1a], Camillo[1a] "Charles," Luigi[1a], Marco[1a], Rocco[1a], Genoeffa[1a], Gelsumina[1a], Adolpho[1a] "Adolfo" and Brigida[1a].

The Dovel Family

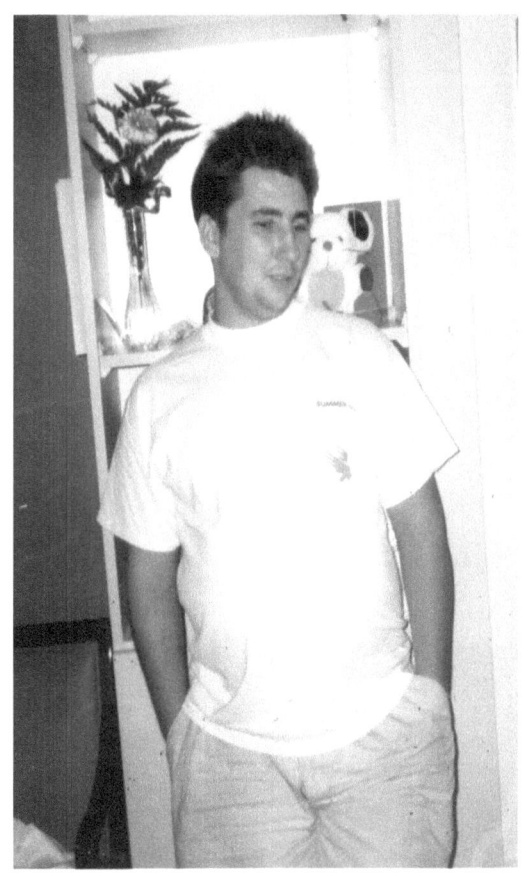

Ronald Hilton Dovel

The Life and Times of
Ronald Hilton[8] Dovel

PATERNAL ANCESTRY: [DOVEL: Richard Harvey[7], Carl Sylvester[6], William Tazewell[5], Peter Simon[4], William[3], David S.[2], Jr., David S.[1] {of England}]

MATERNAL ANCESTRY: [ALTIZER: Wanda Jean[8], Roy Cecil Riley[7], William Fulton[6], Riley A.[5], William A.[4], David Riley[3], Emerich[2], Johan Peter[1] {Althauser of Segendorff, Germany}, Wilmhelm[2a], Jacob[2a]]

RONALD HILTON[8] was born on June 30, 1964 at Winchester, Frederick County, Virginia. His father was Richard Harvey[7] Dovel of Stephens City, Frederick County, Virginia. His mother was Wanda Jean[8] Altizer of Tazewell County, Virginia.

RONALD HILTON[8] married, first, Sharon Lynn "Sheri" Westover on January 3, 1984 at Winchester, Frederick County, Virginia. They divorced on May 2, 1991 at Winchester, Frederick County, Virginia. She was born on September 15, 1953 in West Virginia. Her father was Don Alden Westover of Frederick County, Virginia. Her mother was Betty Leadbetter.

Sharon married, second, Philip Lee McBride on November 1, 2005 at Winchester, Frederick County, Virginia. Issue, if any, is not known.

Ronald Hilton Dovel & Elizabeth Ann Battani Wedding Ceremony

RONALD HILTON[8] married, second, Elizabeth Ann[3] Battani on May 25, 1991 at Great Falls, Fairfax County, Virginia. They were divorced on August 11, 1997 at Statesville, Iredell County, North Carolina. She was born on August 31, 1972 at San Jose, Santa Clara County, California. Her father was Charles Anton[2] [Theodore Joseph[1] {of Modena, Italy}, Camillo[1a] "Charles," Ricardo[2a], Luigi[3a]] Battani of Madrid, Boone County, Iowa. Her mother was Kathryn Aileen "Kay" [Tilford Oliver Monroe "Tom" {of Kentucky, whose wife was Hazel Beaver of Olympia, Washington, daughter of Al Beaver}] Bennett of San Francisco, California.

Elizabeth Ann[3] married, second, Christopher Philip[11] Colson on September 16, 1997 at Statesville, Iredell County, North Carolina. Elizabeth[3] and Christopher[11] were divorced on June 30, 2005 at Pasquotank County, North Carolina. He was born on July 6, 1970 in the Calambrone Military Hospital at Pisa, Tuscany, Italy. His biological father was Philip Alan[5] [Leo

Francis[4], Oscar Joseph[3], Ernest Albert[2], William[1] {of England}, (Mary[1a] or Sarah[1a]), George[2a], Friend[3a]] Coleman of Landover, Prince Georges County, Maryland. His adoptive father was Stanton Darnbrook[10] [Douglas Herman[9], Henry Wilson[8], Stanton E(phraim)[7], Theophilus T.[6] 2nd, Ephraim[5], Ichabod Downs[4], Hatevil[3], Samuel[2], Cornelius[1], Jan Cornelissen[1a] Van Rotterdam {of Rotterdam, Holland}, Cornelius Jonkers[2a]] Colson of Cambridge, Middlesex County, Massachusetts. His mother was Donna Marie[5] [Robert Charles[4], Joseph Francis[3], John Joseph[2], John[1] {of Ireland}]] Higgins of Washington, D. C. Elizabeth[3] and Christopher[11] had two children: Quinn Higgins[12] and Charles Darnbrook[12].

Elizabeth Ann[3] married, third, Wolfgang[1] Murlebach on October 18, 2014 at Port St. Lucie, St. Lucie County, Florida in the office of the County Clerk of the Circuit Court Annex. Wolfgang[1] was born on March 9, 1966 in Germany. The name of his father and mother is not known.

Wolfgang[1] had married, first, Maria Nella Ortiz. Their divorce was recorded on March 15, 2010 at Stuart, Stuart County, Florida.

RONALD HILTON[8] married, third, Debra "Debi" Coffman on May 12, 2000 at Winchester, Frederick County, Virginia by the Justice of the Peace. She was born on August 3, 1957 in Frederick County, Virginia. Her father was Allen Eldridge Coffman of Virginia. Her mother was Elsie Williams of Arkansas. Ronald[8] and Debi had no issue [Editor's Note: However, he is raising her children and one grandchild by Debi's first marriage]. Ronald[8] and Debi currently [2015] live at Inwood, Berkeley County, West Virginia.

Debi had married, first, (Unknown) Fries. Debi and (Unknown) Fries had four children: Matthew, Mary, Bridgett and Sarah

The Children of
Ronald Hilton[8] Dovel
and Sharon Lynn "Sheri" Westover

1. Katie Lynn[9] Dovel
   born on January 5, 1987 at Winchester, Frederick County, Virginia. She married Tyrone Keith Buchanan, Junior on May 19, 2012 in Frederick County, Virginia.

The Children of
Ronald Hilton[8] Dovel
and Elizabeth Ann[3] Battani

2. Dakota Orion[9] Dovel

Ronald Hilton Dovel and son Dakota Orion Dovel

born on December 14. 1992 in the Reston Hospital Center at Reston, Fairfax County, Virginia. He graduated in June 2010 from Northeastern High School at Elizabeth City, Pasquotank County, North Carolina, where he participated all four years in the NHS Air Force Jr. ROTC program, finishing up as President of the Cadet Program and Cadet Lt. Colonel. He married Erica Christine McPhee on June 19, 2015 in the Norfolk Botanical Gardens at Norfolk, Hampton Roads, Virginia. Erica was born on October 3, 1972 at Virginia Beach, Hampton Roads, Virginia. Her father was Eric Christopher McPhee of Norfolk, Hampton Roads, Virginia. Her mother was Judy Lynn Scarbro of Virginia Beach, Hampton Roads, Virginia. They currently [2015] reside at Virginia Beach, Hampton Roads, Virginia.

3. Jacob Michael[9] Dovel

Ronald Hilton Dovel and son Jacob Michael Dovel

born on February 18, 1996 at Reno, Washoe County, Nevada. In 2007 and 2008 he was a member of the River Road Middle School golf team. In 2009/2010 he was attending the 9th grade at Northeastern High School at Elizabeth City, Pasquotank County, North Carolina, where he was a member of the NHS Air Force Jr. ROTC program and a member of the golf team. In 2011 he moved with his mother to Port St. Lucie, St. Lucie County, Florida. He graduated in 2013 from St. Lucie High School, where he finished as a Cadet Lt. Colonel in their Army Jr. ROTC program. He is currently [2015] an Airman Second Class and Assistant Crew Chief in the U. S. Air Force main-tenancing A-10 Warthog ground support jet aircraft at Moody Air Force Base at Valdosta, Lowndes County, Georgia. He is engaged to marry Cadlynne Dunhill in the Spring of 2016.

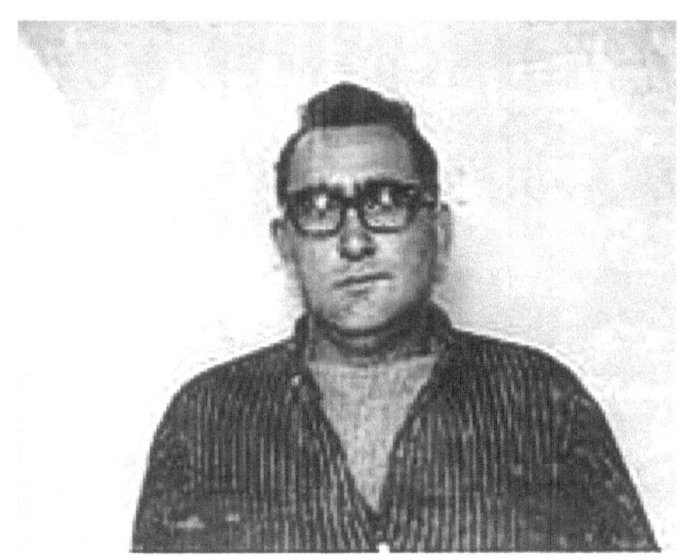

Richard Harvey Dovel

The Life and Times of
Richard Harvey[7] Dovel

PATERNAL ANCESTRY: [DOVEL: Carl Sylvester[6], William Tazewell[5], Peter Simon[4], William[3], David S.[2], Jr., David S.[1] {of England}]

MATERNAL ANCESTRY: [KLINE: Alice Elva, Harvey Enoch, Alexander B., Daniel, John]

RICHARD HARVEY[7] was born on February 19, 1935 at Stephens City, Frederick County, Virginia. He died in a tractor-trailer accident on July 20, 1966 at Gaylord, Clarke County, Virginia and was buried in Mt. Hebron Cemetery at Winchester, Frederick County, Virginia. His father was Carl Sylvester[6] Dovel of Stanley, Page County, Virginia. His mother was Alice Elva Kline of Old Forge, Page County, Virginia.

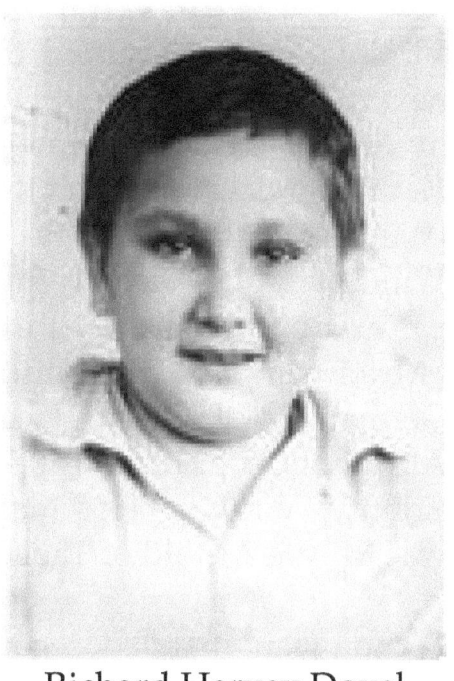

Richard Harvey Dovel
age 6

71

Richard Harvey Dovel

RICHARD HARVEY[7] married Wanda Jean[8] Altizer on June 9, 1956 at Hagerstown, Washington County, Maryland. She was born on November 29, 1940 at Richlands, Tazewell County, Virginia. She died of lung cancer on Friday, October 22, 2010 in the Winchester Memorial Hospital at Winchester, Frederick County, Virginia and was buried there next to Richard Harvey[7] Dovel in Mount Hebron Cemetery. Her father was Roy Cecil Riley[7] [William Fulton[6], Riley A.[5], William A.[4], David Riley[3], Emerich[2], Johan Peter[1] {Althauser of Segendorff, Germany}, Wilmhelm[1a], Jacob[2a]] Altizer of Cedar Bluff, Tazewell County, Virginia. Her mother was Myrtle Arnold of Tazewell County, Virginia.

Wanda Jean Altizer

Wanda Jean[8] married, second, Harvey Lee DeSchon circa 1968/1969 at Winchester, Frederick County, Virginia by the Justice of the Peace. He was born on January 19, 1933 at Winchester, Frederick County, Virginia. He died on September 25, 2003 at Minnesota

City, Winona County, Minnesota and was buried in Section 16, Site 260b at Ft. Snelling National Cemetery at South Minneapolis, Hennepin County, Minnesota. The name of his father is not known. His mother was Lena M. Carpenter. Harvey was a PFC in the U. S. Army and served in both Korea and Viet Nam. Wanda Jean[8] and Harvey had one child: Roy Heath [Editor's Note: Harvey left his family just prior to the birth of his son].

Wanda Jean[8] married, third, David Allan[8] Mason on November 26, 1971 at the United Methodist Church at Winchester, Frederick County, Virginia. He was born on November 8 [another record says November 15], 1943 in the Winchester Memorial Hospital at Winchester, Frederick County, Virginia. His father was Lester Douglas[7] [David Henry[6], Jonathan M.[5], Jonathan L.[4], Jonathan Bingley[3], Andrew[2], George[1] {of Scotland}] Mason of Cross Junction, Frederick County, Virginia. His mother was Ethel V. [Claude E.] Hawkins of Shawnee, Frederick County and later of Clarke County, Virginia. Wanda Jean[8] and David[8] had two children: Carlynn Jean[9] and Cartina Michelle[9] "Tina".

David Allan[8] had a child by Wynnitta (Unknown) [possibly Jones]: Carlotta Mae.

Wanda Jean[8]'s obituary was recorded by the funeral home as follows:

Obituary for Wanda Mason-Altizer

Wanda Jean Mason-Altizer, of Stephens City, beloved wife, mother, grandmother and great grandmother, passed away on Friday, October 22, 2010. She is survived by her husband, David A. Mason, daughters, Carlotta M. Meyer and husband, Donald, Carlynn J. Mason-Scott and husband, Steve, Cartina Mason-Snider and husband, David, and her sons Richard H. Dovel, Robert H. Dovel and wife, Joy, Randall H. Dovel, Ronald H. Dovel and wife, Debra, and Roy DeSchon, as well as her brother, Paul Altizer of Florida. She also leaves behind thirty-two grandchildren and seventeen great grandchildren, all of whom were the joys of her life.

Wanda was preceded in death by her first husband, Richard H. Dovel, her second husband, Harvey DeSchon, and by both of her parents, as well as two of her brothers and four sisters.

Being a lifelong resident of the Winchester area gave Wanda the opportunity to make countless friends and acquaintances, who will miss her and remember her fondly. She was a long-time member and employee of the Berryville Moose Lodge, a dedicated employee of the Sempeles family, as well as Cameron Cleaners in Winchester.

It was the simple pleasures that brought fulfillment to Wanda's life. Love of family and good friends, pride in her Native American heritage and dedication to her work, made her a woman of substance and worth remembering with love and admiration.

The family will receive friends on Wednesday evening from 6:00-8:00 p.m. at the funeral home in Winchester. Loving services will be held at 1:00 p.m. on Thursday, October 28, 2010 at the funeral home. In lieu of flowers, a donation to her burial fund is most sincerly appreciated and can be sent c/o Jones Funeral Home 288 S. Pleasant Valley Rd, Winchester VA 22601.

RICHARD HARVEY[7]'s death was recorded in the *Winchester Star* newspaper as follows:

Father of Four Killed in Crash

Richard Harvey Dovel, 29, father of four children, of Underwood Lane, was killed early this morning when the tractor-trailer he was driving plunged down a 50-ft. embankment.

The accident occurred at 1 a.m. on Route 340 at Gaylord in Clarke County.

State Trooper G. N. Jenkins said Dovel was proceeding north on Route 350, when he went off the left side of the road and down the embankment.

The victim was thrown from the cab and pinned under the tractor, the trooper said. Investigation is continuing.

Dr. James R. York, Clarke County coroner, pronounced him dead at the scene of the accident.

The tractor trailer was owned by the J&L Lines. Trooper Jenkins estimated the damage at $10,000.

He married Wanda Altizer in Hagarstown, Md., on June 9, 1957. They have four sons, Richard H., Jr. Robert H., Randall H., and Ronald H. Dovel, all at home.

Other survivors are the following brothers and sisters: Carl J. Dovel of Oahu, Hawaii; William Dovel of California; Rosetta Blair and Patsy Lake, both of Kernstown, Elva Alt of this city, Janet Sideris and Elsie Herrell of Washington.

He was a member of the Sacred Heart Catholic Church.

The funeral arrangements are incomplete. The body is at the Jones Funeral Home.

The Children of
Richard Harvey[7] Dovel
and Wanda Jean[8] Altizer

1. Richard Harvey[8] "Ricky" Dovel, Jr.
   born on October 3, 1958 in the Winchester
   Memorial Memorial Hopsital at Winchester,
   Frederick County, Virginia. He married Brenda
   Laverne (Unknown). She was born on June 19,
   1952, possibly in Florida. She died, age 57, on
   Saturday, January 2, 2010 at Loganville, Gwinnett
   County, Georgia. Richard[8] and Brenda had one
   child: Angela[9] [who married (Unknown) Nygaard.

   Brenda had married, first, (Unknown) Strickland.
   Brenda and (Unknown) Strickland had two
   children: Don and Kim.

2. Robert Hunter[8] "Bobby" Dovel
   born on November 8, 1961 in the Winchester
   Memorial Hospital at Winchester, Frederick
   County, Virginia. He married Angie Belford on
   December 1, 198X [exact year not known]. She was
   born on December 1, 1963 in Virginia. Her father
   was Robert L. "Bobby" Belford. Her mother was
   Barbara Wallace. Robert[8] and Angie had three
   children: Amanda Ray[9], Robert Hunter[9], Alyssa
   Paige[9].

Robert[8] married, second, Joy Zito of Howard Beach, Queens County, New York. Robert[8] currently [2012] lives in Stephens City, Frederick County, Virginia.

3. Randall Haven[8] "Randy" Dovel
born on October 24, 1962 in the Winchester Memorial Hospital at Winchester, Frederick County, Virginia. He married Susan E. Keifer on July 2, 1989 at Canton, Stark County, Ohio. They were divorced on November 18, 1992 in Stark County, Ohio. She was born on May 11, 1965 in Stark County, Ohio. After their divorce Susan remained at Massillion, Stark County, Ohio. Randy[8] is currently residing [2010] in Louisville, Jefferson County, Kentucky. Randy[8] and Susan had one child: Haven Keifer[9].

4. **Ronald Hilton[8] Dovel**
born on June 30, 1964 in Frederick County, Virginia. He married, first, Sharon Lynn "Sheri" Westover on January 3, 1984 at Winchester, Frederick County, Virginia. They were divorced on May 2, 1991 at Winchester, Frederick, County, Virginia. She was born on September 15, 1953 in West Virginia. Her father was Don Alden Westover of Frederick County, Virginia. Her mother was Betty Leadbetter. Ronald[8] and Sharon had one child: Katie Lynn[9].

Ronald[8] married, second, Elizabeth Ann[3] Battani on May 25, 1991 at Great Falls, Fairfax County, Virginia. They were divorced on August 11, 1997 at Statesville, Iredell County, North Carolina. Elizabeth[3] was born on on August 31, 1972 at San Jose, Santa Clara County, California. Her father was Charles Anton[2] [Theodore Joseph[1] {of Modena, Italy}, Camillo[1a] "Charles", Ricardo[2a], Luigi[3a]] Battani of Madrid, Boone County, Iowa. Her mother was Kathryn E. "Kay" [Tom {of Kentucky, whose wife was Hazel Beaver of Olympia, Washington, daughter of Al Beaver}] Bennett of San Francisco, California. Ronald[8] and Elizabeth[3] had two children: Dakota Orion[9] and Jacob Michael[9].

Ronald[8] married, third, Debra "Debi" Coffman on May 12, 2000 at Winchester, Frederick County, Virginia by the Justice of the Peace. She was born on August 3, 1957 in Frederick County, Virginia. Her father was Allen Eldridge Coffman of Virginia. Her mother was Elsie Williams of Arkansas. Ronald[8] and Debi had no issue.

Debi married, first, (Unknown) Fries. Debi and (Unknown) Fries had four children: Matthew, Mary, Bridgett and Sarah.

Carl Sylveter Dovel

The Life and Times of
Carl Sylvester[6] Dovel

PATERNAL ANCESTRY: [DOVEL: William Tazewell[5], Peter Simon[4], William[3], David S.[2], Jr., David S.[1] {of England}]

MATERNAL ANCESTRY: [HOUSDEN: Leah Hillary Catherine[5], Perry H.[4], Benjamin Dovel[3], Judith[2] {mother}, Benjamin[1] {of Lambeth, England}, William[1a]]

CARL SYLVESTER[6] was born on September 19, 1896 at Stanley, Page County, Virginia. He died of a heart attack circa 1939 at Stephens City, Frederick County, Virginia. His father was William Tazewell[5] Dovel of Page County, Virginia. His mother was Leah Hilary Catherine[5] Housden of Page County, Virginia.

CARL SYLVESTER[6] married, first, Julia Ann[11] Short, she age 16, on December 14, 1914 in Page County, Virginia. They were divorced on June 21, 1919 in Page County, Virginia. She was born on July 15, 1898 at Marksville, Page County, Virginia. She died on November 14, 1972 at Oxon Hill, Prince Georges County, Maryland. Her father was Edward Homer[10] [John A.[9], Amazon L.[8], Richard[7], Wyley[6] {of Brunswick County, Georgia}, John[5] {of Granville County, North Carolina}, William[4] {of Louisa, St.

Georges Parish, Surry County, Virginia}, William[3], William[2], William[1] {of England}, Edward[1a] {Shorte of Brewood, Staffordshire, England}]] Short of Page County, Virginia. Her mother was Barbara Ann [Wesley, Henry, William {of Madison County, Virginia}, Thomas, John] Cubbage of Blue Ridge, Page County, Virginia.

Julia Ann[11] married, second, Stage Arthur Viands on March 5, 1920 in Page County, Virginia. He was born on April 1, 1883 at Old Forge, Page County, Virginia. He died in June 1963 at Luray, Page County, Virginia. His father was Joshua B. [William, Thomas {of Augusta County, Virginia}, John Henry {of Jefferson County, West Virginia}, John A., Thomas, Thomas, John] Viands of Shenandoah County, Virginia. His mother was Elizabeth Melvina [George W., Thomas {of Augusta County, Virginia}, John Henry {of Jefferson County, West Virginia}, John A., Thomas, Thomas, John] Viands of Old Forge, Page County, Virginia. Julia Ann[11] and Stage had six children: (child), Alma, Gladys, Hazel Lee, James Franklin and Stage Arthur, Jr.

Carl Sylvester Dovel and Alice Elva Kline

CARL SYLVESTER[6] married, second, Alice Elva[5] Kline sometime before 1924 [when their first child was born] in Frederick County, Virginia. She was born on January 22, 1904 in Frederick County, Virginia. She died on May 25, 1962 at Winchester, Frederick County, Virginia. Her father was Harvey Enoch[4] [Alexander B.[3], Daniel William[2], John Jacob[1] {Klein of Germany}, Nikolaus[1a] (of Hechtsteim, Mainz, Rheinland-Pfalz, Germany}, Johann Nikolaus[2a] {born 1669}] Kline of Frederick County, Virginia. Her mother was Cora Belle [Enoch Ashby "Ned," Henry Greenfield, John, Lawrence {of St. Mary's County, Maryland}, John] Walters of Frederick County, Virginia.

Alice[5] married, second, Arthur Jackson Lake on June 7, 1946 in Frederick County, Virginia. He was born on February 26, 1893 at Strasburg, Shenandoah County, Virginia. He died on October 19, 1957 at Winchester, Frederick County, Virginia and was buried in the Riverview Cemetery at Strasburg, Shenandoah County, Virginia. His father was Jordan Gabriel [Vincent, Elias {of Fauquier County, Virginia}, Vincent {of St. Mary's, St. Mary's County, Maryland}, William, John] Lake of Rappahannock County, Virginia. His mother was Elizabeth Jane [Henry] Burner of Shenandoah County, Virginia. Alice[5] and Arthur had one child: Patricia Marie.

Arthur had married, first, Florence Ophelia[6] Orndorff sometime before 1926 [when their son Jack was born] in Frederick County, Virginia. She was born on March 24, 1904 at Strasburg, Shenandoah County, Virginia. She died on December 27, 1932 at Winchester, Frederick County, Virginia. Her father was Phillip Madison[5] [Benjamin A.[4], Samuel[3] {of Gravel Springs, Frederick County, Virginia}, Benjamin[2], Johannes Peter[1] {of Burbach, Erftkreis, Northern-Westfalen, Germany}, Peter Henrich[1a], Matthias[2a], Ludwig[3a], Hubert[4a], Henn Zu[5a], Simon Zu[6a] {born 1544 of Hof Orndorff, Bayern, Germany}] Orndorff of Virginia. Her mother was Mary Ann [Jeremiah {of Hardy County, West Virginia}] Sager of Shenandoah County, Virginia. Arthur and Florence[6] had three children: Jack Haywood, Curtis and Thelma Allen.

CARL SYLVESTER[6] registered for the draft [World War I] on June 1, 1917. The registration card says that he was laborer with the R&N Railroad Company in Shenandoah, Virginia. At that time he was single with no dependents, Caucasian, was tall and of medium build, had gray eyes and had light brown hair.

The Children of
Carl Sylvester[6] Dovel
and Julia Ann[11] Short

1. Edward R.[7] Dovel
   born in March 1917 in Page County, Virginia. His
   date and place of death is not known.

2. Elmira Virginia[7] Dovel
   born in August 1918 in Page County, Virginia. Her
   date and place of death is not known.

The Children of
Carl Sylvester[6] Dovel
and Alice Elva[5] Kline

3. Catherine B.[7] Dovel
   born circa 1924 at Stephens City, Frederick County,
   Virginia. Her date and place of death is not known.

4. William Sylvester[7] Dovel
   born on October 5, 1925 at Stephens City, Frederick
   County, Virginia. He died on November 29, 1974
   at Los Angeles [city of], California.

5. Elsie V.[7] Dovel
   born circa 1927 at Stephens City, Frederick County,
   Virginia. She married (Unknown) Herrell of Frederick County, Virginia [Editor's Note: She may be

one in the same person as Elsie V. Herrell who was born on November 11, 1926 in Virginia and who died on November 18, 2004 in Washington, D. C.].

6. Carl J.[7] Dovel
   born on March 2, 1928 at Stephens City, Frederick County, Virginia. He died on December 4, 1985 Ventura, Ventura County, California. He married Lovada Dick. The date and place of their marriage is not known. The were divorced in February 1972 at Ventura, Ventura County, Georgia. She was born circa 1927 in Colorado [another record says Indiana]. Her father and mother may have been Walter A. Dick of Indiana and Minnie M. (Unknown) of Georgia. Carl[7] served in the U. S. Navy aboard the aircraft carrier *Boxer* — sail date was June 25, 1947. Issue, if any, is not known.

7. Anna Rosetta[7] Dovel
   born on February 18, 1930 at Stephens City, Frederick County, Virginia. She died on January 21, 1998 at Winchester, Frederick County, Virginia. She married Charles Edward[6] Blair. The date and place of their marriage is not known. He was born on February 3, 1932 in Texas. He died on August 21, 1995 at Winchester, Frederick County, Virginia. His father was Oscar M.[5] [James M. D.[4], William Soloman[3], John Soloman[2] {of Newberry, Newberry County, South Carolina}, David[1] {of Ireland},

William[1a] {of Ulster Province, Ireland}, Samuel[2a] {of Ballyvoy, Antrim, Ireland}, Daniel[3a] {of Ralloo, Antrim, Ireland}, Brice[4a] {of Blair, Ayershire, Ireland}] Blair of Pike County, Alabama. His mother was Elsie Halliday of Alabama. Anna[7] and Charles[6] had one child: Bonnita[7].

8. **Richard Harvey[7] Dovel**

born on February 19, 1935 at Stephens City, Frederick County, Virginia. He died in a tractor-trailer accident on July 20, 1966 at Gaylord, Clarke County, Virginia and was buried in Mt. Hebron Cemetery at Winchester, Frederick County, Virginia. He married Wanda Jean[8] Altizer on June 9, 1956 at Hagarstown, Washington County, Maryland. She was born on November 29, 1940 at Richlands, Tazewell County, Virginia. She died on Friday, October 22, 2010 at Winchester, Frederick County, Virginia and was buried there next to Richard[7]. Her father was Roy Cecil Riley[7] [William Fulton[6], Riley A.[5], William A.[4], David Riley[3], Emerich[2], Johan Peter[1] {Althauser of Segendorff, Germany}, Wilmhelm[1a], Jacob[2a]] Altizer of Cedar Bluff, Tazewell County, Virginia. Her mother was Myrtle Arnold of Tazewell County, Virginia. Richard[7] and Wanda Jean[8] had four children: Richard Harvey[8] "Ricky", Robert Hunter[8] "Bobby", Randy Haven[8] and Ronald Hilton[8].

Wanda Jean[8] married, second, Harvey Lee DeSchon circa 1968/1969 at Winchester, Frederick County, Virginia by the Justice of the Peace. He was born on January 19, 1933 at Winchester, Frederick County, Virginia. He died on September 25, 2003 at Minnesota City, Winona County, Minnesota and was buried in Section 16, Site 260b at Ft. Snelling National Cemetery at South Minneapolis, Hennepin County, Minnesota. The name of his father is not known. His mother was Lena M. Carpenter. Harvey was a PFC in the U. S. Army and served in both Korea and Viet Nam. Wanda Jean[8] and Harvey had one child: Roy Heath.

Wanda Jean[8] married, third, David Allan[8] Mason on November 26, 1971 at the United Methodist Church at Winchester, Frederick County, Virginia. He was born on November 8, 1943 in the Winchester Memorial Hospital at Winchester, Frederick County, Virginia. His father was Lester Douglas[7] [David Henry[6], Jonathan M.[5], Jonathan L.[4], Jonathan Bingley[3], Andrew[2], George[1] {of Scotland}] Mason of Cross Junction, Frederick County, Virginia. His mother was Ethel V. [Claude E.] Hawkins of Shawnee, Frederick County and later of Clarke County, Virginia. Wanda Jean[8] and David[8] had two children:

a. Carlynn Jean[9] Mason

   born on June 13, 1972 in the Winchester Memorial Hospital at Winchester, Frederick County, Virginia. She married Steven Scott in Stephens City, Virginia. Carlynn[9] and Steven had three children; Aubrey Jean, Rachael Ann and Joshua Steven.

b. Cartina Michelle[9] "Tina" Mason

   born on November 29, 1974 in the Winchester Memorial Hospital at Winchester, Frederick County, Virginia. She married David Andrew Snider on May 28, 1994 at Sherando Park, Stephens City, Frederick County, Virginia. He was born on January 9, 1973 in the Winchester Memorial Hospital at Winchester, Frederick County, Virginia. His father was Henry Snider of Frederick County, Virginia. His mother was Brenda (Unknown) of Frederick County, Virginia. Cartina[9] and David had eight children: Brittney Nicole [born July 15, 1994], Zakkery Orion [born August 20, 1995], Ashleigh Michel [born January 5, 1997], Daniel Branson [born January 28, 1999], Elijah Allan [born April 28, 2001], Isaiah Adam [born April 30, 2006], Taylorann Grace [born April 28, 2009] and Madeleine Jean [born January 28, 2012], all born in Winchester, Frederick County, Virginia.

The Life and Times of
William Tazewell[5] Dovel

PATERNAL ANCESTRY: [DOVEL: Peter Simon[4], William[3], David S.[2], Jr., David S.[1] {of England}]

MATERNAL ANCESTRY: [HOUSER: Hannah Rebecca, Nicholas]

WILLIAM TAZEWELL[5] was born on March 8, 1866 at East Liberty, Page County, Virginia. He died sometime after 1930 [when he last appears on the U.S. Census, age 64] in Page County, Virginia. His father was Peter Simon[4] Dovel of Page or Rockingham County, Virginia. His mother was Hannah Rebecca Houser of Page County, Virginia.

WILLIAM TAZEWELL[5] married Leah Hillary Catherine[5] [also found as Jean Hillary] Housden on January 26, 1892 at Alma, Page County, Virginia. She was born in 1874 in Page County, Virginia. She died in 1920 in Page County, Virginia. Her father was Perry H.[4] [Benjamin Dovel[3], Judith[2] {of Culpeper County, Virginia {{Note: John Dovel (ancestry unknown) was his natural father; however, Benjamin took his mother's Housden surname}}, Benjamin[1] {of Lambeth, London, England}, William[1a] {of Bigglewade, Bedfordshire, England}] Housden of Honeyville, Page County, Virginia. Her mother was Mary

Catherine [Matthew {of Hawksbill, Shenandoah County, Virginia}, Levi, Matthew] Lucas of Page County, Virginia.

The Children of William Tazewell[5] Dovel and Leah Hillary Catherine[5] Housden

1. Maggie L.[6] Dovel
   born circa June 1892 in Page County, Virginia. Her date and place of death is not known She last appears on the 1910 U. S. Census, age 18, living at home in Page County, Virginia [Editor's Note: There was a Margaret Dovel born on May 14, 1892 in Virginia and died in June 1985 at Great Falls, Fairfax County, Virginia, who may be one in the same person].

2. Lena Gertrude[6] Dovel
   born on February 2, 1894 in Page County, Virginia. She died on August 7, 1971 at Shenandoah, Page County, Virginia. She married Chelous Harold[7] Austin in 1918 in Page County, Virginia. He was born on August 19, 1895 at Shenandoah, Page County, Virginia. He died on July 28, 1986 at Shenandoah, Page County, Virginia. His father was John Henry[6] [John H.[5] {of Spotsylvania County, Virginia}, Richard[4], Henry[3] {of Calvert County, Maryland}, Samuel[2], Henry[1] {of Shevlock,

Cornwall, England}, Thomas[1a], Thomas[2a]] Austin of Page County, Virginia. His mother was Mary Jane[6] [Henry[5], Peter[4] {of Shenandoah County, Virginia, George[3] {of Frederick County, Virginia}, Johann Heinrich[2] {Bentz of Iggleheim, Pfalz, Baveim, Germany and later of Mad River, Champaign Countu, Ohio}, Johan Georg[1] {Bentz of Iggleheim, Pfalz, Baveim, Germany and later of Shenandoah County, Virginia}] Pence of Page County, Virginia. Lena[6] and Chelous[7] had six children:

a. Helen Janice[8] Austin
    born on August 31, 1918 at Shenandoah, Page County, Virginia. She died, age 84, on May 15, 2003 in her home at Madison, Madison County, Virginia and was buried in Eastlawn Memorial Gardens at Harrisonburgh, Rockingham County, Virginia. She married William James Gardiner. He was born on March 6, 1910 in Frederick County, Virginia. He died on December 6, 1968 at Elkton, Rockingham County, Virginia. His father was Charles Walter [Isaac John, William S., George {born 1774 in Virginia}] Gardner of Frederick County, Virginia. His mother was Alberta E. Durfinger of Virginia. Helen[8] and William had two children: James J. and Julian W.

b. Theo Evelyn[8] "Jackie" Austin
born on December 17, 1920 at Shenandoah,
Page County, Virginia. She died on September
17, 2008 at Shenandoah, Page County, Virginia.
She married Wordell [afa Wardell] Arnold
Stanley on May 28, 1938 in Page County,
Virginia. He was born on January 29, 1915 at
Shenandoah, Page County, Virginia. He died on
November 28, 2002 at Shenandoah, Page
County, Virginia. His father was Luther Martin
[John E., John H.] Stanley of Page County,
Virginia. His mother was Shirley Lee [Henry
Preston, Henry] Comer of Page County,
Virginia. "Jackie[8]" and Wordell had three
children: Allen V., Gloria S. and Rondal V.

c. Paul Charles[8] Austin
born on November 17, 1921 in Frederick
County, Virginia. He died on January 19, 2010
at home in Shenandoah, Page County, Virginia
and was buried there in the Mount Lebanon
Cemetery. He married Catherine Marie[8]
"Boogie" Painter in 1948 in Page County,
Virginia. She was born on September 12, 1929 in
Page County, Virginia. She died on October 19,
2003 in the University of Virginia Medical
Center at Charlottesville, Albemarle County,
Virginia. Her father was Earman Clinton[7]
[Franklin Lewis[6], Peter C.[5], John[4], Peter[3] {of

Botetourt County, Virginia}, Joseph Conrad[2] {of Frederick, Page County, Virginia}, Conrad Bender[1] {of Dishren, Rhein-Neckar-Krels, Baden-Wuerttenberg, Germany}] Painter of Luray, Page County, Virginia. Her mother was Florence [James Amos, William Christopher {of Rockingham County, Virginia}, James {born circa 1781}] Hilliards of Ingram, Page County, Virginia. Paul[8] and Catherine[8] had six children: Paul T.[9], Gary E.[9], Dexter R.[9], Della[9], Roxie Ann[9] and Linda[9].

d. Wiley Hudson[8] Austin
born on January 20, 1924 in Page County, Virginia. He died on February 4, 2003 in the Martinsburg Veteran's Center at Martinsburg, Berkeley County, West Virginia. He was an Army veteran of World War II.

e. Lawrence Jackson[8] Austin
born on April 10, 1929 in Page County, Virginia. He died, age 31, on September 18, 1960 in Page County, Virginia and was buried there in the Rest Haven Cemetery at Shenandoah. He married an unknown person and had one child: name not known.

f. Curtis P.[8] Austin
born sometime after 1930 in Page County,

Virginia. He married Betty Jean May on March 8, 1952 in Page County, Virginia. She was born on July 18, 1937 at Shenandoah, Page County, Virginia. She died on October 14, 1977 in the University of Virginia Medical Center at Charlottesville, Albemarle County, Virginia and was buried in the Rest Haven Cemetery at Shenandoah, Page County, Virginia. Her father was Paul Albert [William Oscar {of Rockingham County, Virginia}, James Daniel, Jacob] May of Page County, Virginia. Her mother was Zethel Marie [Amos Clifton, George W.] Weaver of Page County, Virginia. Curtis[8] and Betty had five children: three whose names are not known, and (son)[9] and Jeffrey Lynn[9].

3. **Carl Sylvester[6] Dovel**
   born on September 19, 1896 at Stanley, Page County, Virginia. He died of a heart attack circa 1939 at Stephens City, Frederick County, Virginia. He married, first, Julia Ann[11] Short, she age 16, on December 14, 1914 in Page County, Virginia. They were divorced on June 21, 1919 in Page County, Virginia. She was born on July 15, 1898 at Marksville, Page County, Virginia. She died on November 14, 1972 at Oxon Hill, Prince Georges County, Maryland. Her father was Edward Homer[10] [John A[9]., Amazon L.[8], Richard[7], Wyley[6] {of Brunswick County, Georgia}, John[5] {of Granville County, North Carolina}, William[4] {of

98

Louisa, St. George Parish, Surry County, Virginia, William[3], William[2], William[1] {of England}, Edward[1a] {of Shorte of Breewood, Staffordshire, England] Short of Page County, Virginia. Her mother was Barbara Ann [Wesley, Henry, William {of Madison County, Virginia}, Thomas, John] Cubbage of Blue Ridge, Page County, Virginia. Carl[6] and Julia[11] had two children: Edward R.[7] and Elmira Virginia[7].

Carl[6] married, second, Alice Elva[5] Kline sometime before 1924 [when their first child was born] in Frederick County, Virginia. She was born on January 22, 1904 in Frederick County, Virginia. She died on May 25, 1962 at Winchester, Frederick County, Virginia. Her father was Harvey Enoch[4] [Alexander B.[3], Daniel William[2], John Jacob[1] {Klein of Germany}, Nikolaus[1a] {of Hechtsteim, Mainz, Rheinland-Pfalz, Germany}, Johan Nikolaus[2a] {born circa 1669}] Kline of Frederick County, Virginia. Her mother was Cora Belle [Enoch Ashby "Ned," Henry Greenfield, John, Lawrence {of St. Mary's County, Maryland}, John] Walters of Frederick County, Virginia. Carl[6] and Alice[5] had six children: Catherine B.[7], William S.[7], Elsie V.[7], Carl J.[7], Anna Rosetta[7], Richard Harvey[7].

4. Mamie Mae[6] Dovel
born on May 3, 1900 in Page County, Virginia. She

died on February 22, 1962 at Staunton, Augusta County, Virginia and was buried in the Seekford Family Cemetery at Alma, Page County, Virginia. She married, as his third wife, Jacob Richard[3] Seekford on September 22, 1919 [another record says May 1916, but this is incorrect] in Page County, Virginia. He was born in September 1857 in Page County, Virginia. He died in 1938 at Alma, Page County, Virginia. His father was Richard Adam[2] {sometimes found as Adam Richard[2]} [George Washington[1] {of Germany}] Seekford of Page County, Virginia. His mother was Eliza Jane[3] [David[2], John[1] {of Germany}] Freeze of Shenandoah, Page County, Virginia. Mamie[6] and Jacob[3] had two children:

g. Sarah F.[4] Seekford
    born circa 1920/1922 at Marksville, Page County, Virginia. Her date of death, presumably at Marksville, Page County, Virginia, is not known [probably young, as no further record is found].

h. Calvin Coolidge[4] Seekford [a daughter]
    born on March 4, 1923 [another researcher says 1925] at Marksville, Page County, Virginia. She married Melvin Conrad Housden on March 29, 1947 in Page County, Virginia. He was born on September 15, 1916 at Stanley, Page County,

Virginia. He died on July 29, 1999 in Page Memorial Hospital at Luray, Page County, Virginia and was buried on August 2, 1999 in the Leak's Chapel Church of the Brethren Cemetery at Stanley. His father was George William [James Tazewell William, John, John] Housden of Page County, Virginia. His mother was Della Mae [whose father was unknown and whose mother was Sarry Rhinehart] Rhinehart of Page County, Virginia. Calvin[4] and Melvin had seven children: six whose names are not known and Melvin Conrad.

Jacob[3] had married, first, Ada F. Phillips on May 3, 1883 in Page County, Virginia. Ada was born on April 22, 1863 at Shenandoah Iron Works, Page County, Virginia [another record says New Market, Shenandoah County, Virginia]. They were divorced in 1919. She died, age 77, on February 1, 1941 at Alma, Page County, Virginia. Her father was John Phillips of Virginia. Her mother was Martha Alice of Virginia. Jacob[3] and Ada had three children:

a. Bertie Mae[4] Seekford
born on May 1, 1910 at Marksville Township, Page County, Virginia. She died on May 29, 2005 in a local nursing home at White Post, Clarke County, Virginia and was buried on

June 1, 2005 in the Shenandoah Memorial Park Cemetery at Winchester, Frederick County, Virginia. She married Isaac Gardiner Clark sometime before May 1929 [when their first child was born], presumably in Page County, Virginia. He was born on March 21, 1913 in Virginia. He died on December 13, 1963 in Virginia. His father was Reuben Clark of Virginia. His mother was Hattie Belle [Isaac John, William] Gardiner of Frederick County, Virginia. Bertie[4] and Isaac had three children: Sarah Frances, Gloria and Roger Gardiner.

b. Louise[4] Seekford
born in 1912 at Marksville Township, Page County, Virginia. Her date and place of death is not known. She married (Unknown) Bauserman, who was born circa 1904.

c. Estella Mary[4] Seekford
born in 1913 at Marksville Township, Page County, Virginia. Her date and place of death is not known. She married (Unknown) Miller who was born circa 1912.

Jacob[3] had married, second, Esta [afa Estha] M. Good on August 30, 1917 in Page County, Virginia. She was born on June 4, 1892 in Page County, Virginia. She died [apparently during childbirth] on January 21, 1919 at Stanley, Page County, Virginia and was buried there in the Seekford Family Cemetery at Alma. The name of her father is not known. Her mother was Mary Susan (Unknown) of Virginia. Jacob[3] and Esta had three children:

d. Janie A.[4] Seekford
   born in July 1916 in Page County, Virginia [Editor's Note: This is pure speculation until documentation to refute it is discovered, but this editor believes she was born by Esta prior to Esta's marriage to Jacob[3] and may have been the cause of his divorce from Ada F. Phillips]. She died on May 24, 2002 at White Post, Clarke County, Virginia. Janie[4] married Sandy (Unknown), who was born circa 1914.

e. Jacob Richard[4] Seekford, Jr.
   born in 1917 in Page County, Virginia. He died in 1917 in Page County, Virginia and was buried there in the Seekford Family Cemetery.

f. Adam[4] Seekford
   born in January 1919 in Page County, Virginia. He died on January 21, 1919 in Page County, Virginia and was buried there in the Seekford Family Cemetery.

Mamie Mae[6] married, second, Harry David Courtney on November 2, 1938 in Page County, Virginia. He was born on August 1, 1885 in Page County, Virginia. He died on August 19, 1954 near Stanley, Page County, Virginia and was buried there in the Seekford Family Cemetery at Alma. His father was Benjamin F. Courtney of Page County, Virginia. His mother was Fannie Seal of Page County, Virginia. Issue, if any, is not known.

Harry had married, first, Maude Cecelia[7] Hitt on January 11, 1905 in Page County, Virginia. She was born on July 28, 1887 in Page County, Virginia. She died on July 18, 1936 in Page County, Virginia and was buried there in the United Church of Christ Cemetery in Newport, Page County, Virginia. Her father was William F.[6] [Ludwell[5] {of Culpeper County, Virginia}, James William[4] {of Fauquier County, Virginia}, John[3] {of Prince William County, Virginia}, John[2] {of Germanna, Essex County, Virginia}, Peter[1] {of Kaan-Marienborn, Nassau-Siegen, Westphalia, Germany}, Johan Jacob[1a] {Heite of Rehbach, Siegen, Germany}, Jacob[2a], Balthasar[3a], Hans[4a] {of Marrienborn, Germany}, Johann[5a] {born circa 1540 of Rehbach, Germany}] Hitt of Rappahannock County, Virginia. His mother was Nancy E. [Miller] Cubbage of Rappahannock County, Virginia.

5. Elmer Lynwood[6] Dovel
born on December 5, 1903 in Page County, Virginia. He died on April 8, 1921 in Frederick County, Virginia and was buried there in Ridings Chapel United Methodist Cemetery at Stephens City.

6. Minnie I.[6] Dovel
born circa 1907/1908 in Page County, Virginia. She died on December 5, 1931 at Harrisonburg, Rockingham County, Virginia and was buried there in the Woodbine Cemetery. In 1930 she was living as a servant for the family of Claud R. Connor at Winchester, Frederick County, Virginia.

7. Myrtle V.[6] Dovel
born circa 1911 in Page County, Virginia. Her date and place of death is not known.

8. Russell William[6] Dovel
born on October 4, 1915 in Page County, Virginia. He died on May 3, 1937 in Frederick County, Virginia and was buried there in Ridings Chapel United Methodist Cemetery at Stephens City.

The Life and Times of
Peter Simon[4] Dovel

PATERNAL ANCESTRY: [DOVEL: William[3], David S.[2], Jr., David S.[1] {of England}]

MATERNAL ANCESTRY: [LONG: Christina[4], Mathias[3], Heinrick Emanuel[2], Philip[1] {of Germany}]

PETER SIMON[4] was born on August 8, 1821 in Shenandoah County, Virginia. He died on February 9, 1903 in Page County, Virginia. His father was William[3] Dovel of Alma, Rockingham County, Virginia. His mother was Christina[4] Long of Virginia.

PETER SIMON[4] married, first, Julia Ann Jenkins on November 14, 1850 in Page County, Virginia. She was born circa 1832 in Page County, Virginia. She died sometime before 1860 [when Peter[4] married second] in Page County, Virginia. The name of her father is not known. Her mother was Eula (Unknown) of Page County, Virginia.

PETER SIMON[4] married, second, Hannah Rebecca Houser on March 1, 1860 in Page County, Virginia. She was born on September 5, 1838 in Page County, Virginia. She died on June 15, 1873 at East Liberty, Page County, Virginia. Her father was Nicholas Houser of Pennsylvania. Her mother was Magdalene

[Phillip] Shaffer of Dry Run, Page County, Virginia.

PETER SIMON[4] married, third, Ann Eliza Cubbage on December 24, 1874 in Page County, Virginia. She was born circa 1837/1840 in Page County, Virginia. She died, age 56, of dropsy on September 25 [another record says the 15th], 1895 in Page County, Virginia. Her father was William [Thomas {of Page County, Virginia}, John, Philemon {of Kent, Delaware County, Delaware}, George {born 1680 in Delaware}] Cubbage of Madison County, Virginia. Her mother was Sarah[4] "Sally" [Benjamin[3] {of Culpeper, Culpeper County, Virginia}, William[2], William[1] {of Whitehaven, Cumberland, England}, Thomas[1a]] Nicholson of Madison County, Virginia. Issue, if any, is not known.

The Children of
Peter Simon⁴ Dovel
and Julia Ann Jenkins

1. **Peter Simon⁵ Dovel**
   born on October 26, 1850 in Page County, Virginia.
   He died on January 12, 1938 in Page County,
   Virginia. He married, first, Barbara Elizabeth⁶
   Guchenour on March 10, 1873 in Page County,
   Virginia. She was born about 1853, presumably in
   Shenandoah County, Virginia. Her date and place
   of death is not known. Her father was Joseph⁵
   [Abraham⁴, John³ {of Augusta County, Virginia},
   Jacob², Heinrich¹ "Henry" {Gachenauer of Switz-
   erland}, Joseph¹ᵃ {Gachnawer}, Henrich²ᵃ, Jakob³ᵃ
   {of Fischenthal Parish, Zurich, Switzerland}]
   Guchenour of Shenandoah County, Virginia. Her
   mother was Rebecca Ann [Isaac, Balthasar {Sauer
   of Frederick County, Virginia}, Henry Balzer]
   Sours of Shenandoah County, Virginia. Peter⁵ and
   Barbara Elizabeth⁶ had seven children:

   a. **Mollie Viola⁶ Dovel**
      born on December 12, 1873 near Leaksville,
      Page County, Virginia. Her date and place of
      death is not known.

   b. **Sarah J.⁶ Dovel**
      born in 1874 near Leaksville, Page County,

109

Georgia. She died in childbirth on February 7, 1893 at Luray, Page County, Virginia and was buried there in the Leaksville United Church of Christ Cemetery. She married William Abraham Shenk on may 26, 1892 in Page County, Virginia. He was born on March 9, 1867 at Springfield, Page County, Virginia. He died on January 29, 1923 at Luray, Page County, Virgina and was buried there in the Beahm's Chapel Cemetery. His father was Theodore Franklin [Abraham, John, John] Shenk of Virginia. His mother was Selenas Pocahontas [William H. {of Loudoun County, Virginia}] McCullough of Virginia. Sarah[6] and William had a child who died with her mother at birth.

William married, second, Lula George Jones on May 2, 1894 in Page County, Virginia. She was born on June 17, 1875 in Page County, Virginia. She died on June 26, 1930 in Page County, Virginia. Her father was Isaac Burell Jones of Luray, Page County, Virginia. Her mother was Martha A. "Lucinda" [Adam J. {of Criders, Rockingham County, Virginia}, George Ward, Christopher, Jacob {of Lancaster, Lancaster County, Pennsylvania}, Jacob] Halterman of Rockingham County, Virginia. William and Lula had six children: Alma Margaret, Nanie Beulah, William F., Ernest Floyd, Charles

Milbourne and Laura Myrtle.

c. John W.[6] Dovel
   born on February 12, 1876 near Leaksville, Page County, Virginia. He died sometime before 1903 in Page County, Virginia. He married Rosa E. Eppard on May 21, 1899 in Page County, Virginia. She was born on March 12, 1877 at Leaksville, Page County, Virginia. She died on April 16, 1951 at Baltimore, Baltimore County, Maryland and was buried in the Eppard Family Cemetery at Leaksville, Page County, Virginia. Her father was Samuel B. Eppard of Page County, Virginia. Her mother was Sarah V. Hensley of Page County, Virginia. John[6] and Rosa had no issue.

   Rosa married, second, Robert Theodore Atwood on May 11, 1904 in Page County, Virginia. He was born on June 16, 1877 in Page County, Virginia. He died on January 17, 1929 in Page County, Virginia and was buried there in the Eppard Family Cemetery at Leaksville, Page County, Virginia. His father was Nehemiah [Sinnert, Sinnert, Gilbert {of Westmoreland County, Virginia}, John {born circa 1702}] Atwood of Page County, Virginia. His mother was Mary Catherine [Daniel, David, Christian {of Frederick County, Virginia}, John

Jacob] Bumgardner of Page County, Virginia. Issue, if any, is not known.

Rosa married, third, Leo Leonard Zippler. The date and place of their marriage is not known. He was born on June 19, 1887 [another record says 1888] in Louisville, Jefferson County, Kentucky. He died on November 15, 1958 in Baltimore, Baltimore County, Maryland and was buried there on November 20th in the Baltimore National Cemetery, Section M, Site 1856. The name of his father is not known. His mother was Eva Mary Byerly of Pennsylvania. There was no issue.

d. David A.[6] Dovel
born in 1879 in Page County, Virginia. His date and place of death is not known.

e. Lovenia[6] Dovel
born on September 1880 in Page County, Virginia. She died on November 5, 1957, presumably in Page County, Virginia and was buried there in the Leaksville United Church of Christ Cemetery at Luray. She married Henry David Eppard on September 4, 1902 in Page County, Virginia. He was born on November 1, 1870 in Page County, Virginia. He died on September 16, 1938 in Page County, Virginia

and was buried there in the Leaksville United Church of Christ Cemetery at Luray. His father was James David [Daniel {of Rockingham County, Virginia}] Eppard of Page County, Virginia. His mother was Susan Elizabeth [Alexander {of North Carolina}] Nicholson of Madison County, Virginia. Lovenia[6] and Henry had three children: Floyd William, Neva Marie and Ruth V.

f. Martha Virginia[6] Dovel
    born on March 11, 1885 in Page County, Virginia. She died on November 9, 1967, presumably in Page County, Virginia and was buried there in the Leaksville United Church of Christ Cemetery at Luray. She married John Adams Sours on December 31, 1907 in Page County, Virginia. He was born on September 5, 1873 at Hawksbill, Page County, Virginia. He died on September 11, 1959 at Luray, Page County, Virginia and was buried there in the Leaksville United Church of Christ Cemetery. His father was David [Isaac, Balthasar {Sauer of Frederick County, Virginia}, Henry] Sours of Shenandoah County, Virginia. His mother was Missouri Catherine [John] Thomas of Shenandoah County, Virginia. Martha[6] and John had four children: Ethel Mae, Geneva Pearl, Nina Virginia and Roland John.

g. Isaac Newton[6] Dovel
born in 1888 in Page County, Virginia. He died on May 24, 1898 at Leaksville, Page County, Virginia and was buried there Leaksville United Church of Christ Cemetery.

Peter[5] married, second, Barbara Ann Sours on August 22, 1896 at Page County, Virginia. She was born on December 25, 1870 in Page County, Virginia. She died on April 2, 1903 in Page County, Virginia. Her father was David [Isaac, Balthasar {Sauer of Frederick County, Virginia}, Henry Balzer] Sours of Shenandoah County, Virginia. Her mother was Missouri Catherine [John] Thomas of Shenandoah County, Virginia. Peter[5] and Barbara Ann had four children:

h. Harry Stacy[6] Dovel
born on May 14, 1898 in Page County, Virginia. He died in 1968 in Washington, D.C. He married Elizabeth May Phillips on May 28, 1918 in Page County, Virginia. She was born on June 18, 1900 in Page County, Virginia. She died on May 26, 1985 at Luray, Page County, Virginia and was buried in the Graves Chapel Cemetery at Stanley. Her father was Edward Herbert [William Kemper, Jonathan F., Jake] Phillips of Page County, Virginia. Her mother was Edna Rila [Johnston] Weakley of Page County,

Virginia. Harry[6] and Elizabeth had six children: James F.[7], Nathaniel E.[7], Lina A.[7], Barbara Ann[7], Aleta[7] and Rosemary Elizabeth[7].

i. (child)[6] Dovel
    born in 1901 in Page County, Virginia. Died on August 31, 1903 in Page County, Virginia.

j. Charles[6] Dovel
    born circa 1903 in Page County, Virginia. His date and place of death is not known.

k. Henry[6] Dovel
    born circa 1903 in Page County, Virginia. His date and place of death is not known.

Peter[5] married, third, Annie Eline Price on November 2, 1905 in Page County, Virginia. She was born on December 3, 1873 in Page County, Virginia. She died on December 19, 1967, presumably in Page County, Virginia. Her father was William H. [Elija, Elijah] Price of Page County, Virginia. Her mother was Jeannette[5] [Abraham[4], Abraham[3], Joseph[2] {of Shenandoah County, Virginia}, Abraham[1] {of Switzerland}] Strickler of Page County, Virginia. Peter[5] and Annie had four children:

l. Roy Finter[6] Dovel
    born on March 10, 1909 at Luray, Page County,
    Virginia. He died on January 9, 1995 at New
    Market, Shenandoah County, Virginia and was
    buried in the Leaksville United Church of
    Christ Cemetery at Luray, Page County, Vir-
    ginia. He married Mary (Unknown) in 1925 in
    Page County, Virginia. She was born in 1908 in
    Virginia. Her date and place of death is not
    known. Roy[6] and Mary had a child: name
    unknown.

    Roy[6] married, second, Reba Alice Moyer on July
    6, 1935 in Page County, Virginia. She was born
    on August 3, 1906 in Page County, Virginia. She
    died on September 10, 1958 in Page County,
    Virginia and was buried there in the Leaksville
    United Church of Christ Cemetery at Luray.
    Her father was Andrew Green [Henry C.,
    Henry, Lewis] Moyer of Page County, Virginia.
    Her mother was Flora Alice [Joseph H., Isaac {of
    Shenandoah County, Virginia}, Daniel] Cullers
    of Page County, Virginia. Roy[6] and Reba had a
    child: name unknown.

m. Ada Mae[6] Dovel
    born on September 12, 1912 at Luray, Page
    County, Virginia. She died on November 14,
    1986 at Harrisonburg, Rockingham County,

Virginia and was buried in the Leaksville United Church of Christ Cemetery at Luray, Page County, Virginia. She married Amos Hudson Waters on April 17, 1937 in Page County, Virginia. He was born on June 30, 1913 in Page County, Virginia. He died on August 16, 1979 in Page County, Virginia and was buried there in the Leaksville United Church of Christ Cemetery at Luray. His father was James Ernest [James Henry {of Rappahannock County, Virginia}, James A., Stanfield] Waters of Page County, Virginia. His mother was Adria Susan [John William, William Henry, Peter, Pearson, Michael, Isaac {born circa 1712}] Judd of Page County, Virginia. Ada[6] and Amos had four children: names unknown.

n. Charles Edward[6] Dovel
born on April 30, 1914 at Luray, Page County, Virginia. He died on March 18, 1986 at Harrisonburg, Rockingham County, Virginia and was buried in the Beahm's Chapel Cemetery at Luray, Page County, Virginia. He married Helen Elizabeth Painter on June 12, 1953 in Page County, Virginia. She was born on November 19, 1913 in Page County, Virginia. She died on July 27, 1986 at Luray, Page County, Virginia and was buried there in the Beahm's Chapel Cemetery. Her father was John

Wilton [Peter C., Peter Bender, Peter Bender, Joseph, Conrad, Peter {born 1710}] Painter of Page County, Virginia. Her mother was Mary Ellen [John W., Christopher] Price of Page County, Virginia. There was no issue.

Helen had married, first, Garland Laniard Hilliards in 1929 in Page County, Virginia. He was born on May 25, 1902 in Page County, Virginia. He died on December 12, 1978 in Page County and was buried there in the SDA Cemetery at Stanley. His father was John Thomas Charles Renson {Hilliard of Frederick County, Virginia}, Jacob] Hilliards of Page County, Virginia. His mother was Carrie Lee [James Henry {of Madison County, Virginia}, Augustine {of Rappahannock County, Virginia}, John Smith & Penelope Cubbage] Cubbage of Page County, Virginia. Helen and Garland had four children: two whose names are unknown, and Vincent Julian and Garland Landon.

o. Lena Bell[6] Dovel
born on March 7, 1916 at Luray, Page County, Virginia. She died on January 22, 2011 in Page County, Virginia and was buried there in the Beahm's Chapel Cemetery at Luray. She married James Ralph Waters on April 18, 1936 in Page County, Virginia. He was born on August

4, 1916 at Luray, Page County, Virginia. He died on June 28, 2002 at Luray, Page County, Virginia and was buried there in the Beahm's Chapel Cemetery. His father was James Ernest [James Henry {of Rappahannock County, Virginia}, James A., Stanfield] Waters of Page County, Virginia. His mother was Adria Susan [John William, William Henry, Peter, Pearson, Michael, Isaac {born circa 1712}] Judd of Page County, Virginia. Lena[6] and James had three children: two whose names are unknown and Betty Lou.

The Children of
Peter Simon[4] Dovel
and Hannah Rebecca Houser

2. David Trenton[5] Dovel
   born in 1860 at Alma, Page County, Virginia. He
   died, age 10, in 1870 in Page County, Virginia.

3. Charles Benton[5] Dovel
   born in September 1862 at Alma, Page County,
   Virginia. He died on March 9, 1935 in Page
   County, Virginia. He married Cora Elizabeth
   Rebecca[5] Housden [sister of Leah Hilary[5] who
   married William Tazewell[5] Dovel] circa 1900 in
   Page County, Virginia. Cora[5] was born in February
   1879 [another record says 1885] in Virginia. She
   died on July 25, 1940 in Page County, Virginia and
   was buried there in the Leaks Chapel Church
   Cemetery at Honeyville. Her father was Perry H.[4]
   [Benjamin Dovel[3], Judith[2] {of Culpeper County,
   Virginia {{Note: John Dovel (ancestry unknown)
   was his natural father; however, Benjamin[3] took
   his mother's Housden surname}}, Benjamin[1] {of
   Lambeth, London, England}, William[1a] {of Bigglewade, Bedfordshire, England}] Housden of Honey-
   ville, Page County, Virginia. Her mother was Mary
   Catherine [Matthew {of Hawksbill, Shenandoah
   County, Virginia}, Levi, Matthew] Lucas of Page
   County, Virginia. Charles[5] and Cora[5] had five

children:

a. Amos Sylvestor[6] Dovel
born on September 30, 1899 at Alma, Page County, Virginia. He died on January 22, 1967 in the Page County, Memorial Hospital at Luray, Page County, Virginia and was buried there in the Leaks Chapel Church of the Brethren Cemetery at Stanley. He married Mattie Virginia McCoy in 1930 in Page County, Virginia. She was born on October 22, 1906 in Page County, Virginia. She died on February 1, 1986 in the Elder Care Garden Nursing Home at Charlottesville, Albemarle County, Virginia and was buried in the Leaks Chapel Church of the Brethren Cemetery at Stanley, Page County, Virginia. Her father was Acree McCoy of Page County, Virginia. Her mother was Regina Lucas of Page County, Virginia. Amos[6] and Mattie had seven children: six whose names are unknown and James Kenneth[7].

b. Hubert Lee[6] Dovel
born on August 10, 1904 at Alma, Page County, Virginia. He died on January 17, 1971 in Page County, Virginia and was buried there in the Leaks Chapel Church of the Brethren Cemetery at Stanley. He married Pauline Elizabeth Long sometime before October 1936 [when their first

121

child was born] in Page County, Virginia. She was born on January 5, 1913 in Page County, Virginia. She died on March 23, 1979 in Page County, Virginia and was buried there in the Leaks Chapel Church of the Brethren Cemetery at Stanley. The name of her father and mother is not known. Hubert[6] and Pauline had six children: four whose names are not known, and James Robert[7] and Gary Preston[7].

c. Maude Blanche[6] Dovel
born on July 24, 1907 at Alma, Page County, Virginia. She died on October 2, 1989 in the Camelot Hall Nursing Home at Harrisonburg, Rockingham County, Virginia and was buried in the Adventist Church Cemetery at Stanley, Page County, Virginia. She married Grover Lee Painter on September 7, 1922 in Page County, Virginia. He was born on July 16, 1902 in Page County, Virginia. His father was Hubert Lee Painter of Page County, Virginia. His mother was Sarah Elizabeth Seekford of Page County, Virginia. Maude[6] and Grover had two children: Iva Mae and Angie Elizabeth.

d. Martie Virginia[6] Dovel
born on December 12, 1916 at Shenandoah, Page County, Virginia. She died on May 18, 2005 at the Mont Vue Nursing Home at Luray,

Page County, Virginia. She married Cornelius Floyd Foltz on December 12, 1940 in Page County, Virginia. He was born on December 21, 1904 in Page County, Virginia. He died on January 31, 1978 in the Page County Memorial Hospital at Luray, Page County, Virginia and was buried there in the Seventh Day Adventist Cemetery at Stanley. His father was George Hiram Foltz of Page County, Virginia. His mother was Mary Elizabeth Purdham of Page County, Virginia. Martie[6] and Cornelius had a child: name unknown.

e. William Alfred[6] Dovel
born on June 25, 1923 at Shenandoah, Page County, Virginia. He died on June 15, 2005 in Page County, Virginia and was buried there in the Evergreen Memory Gardens Cemetery. He married Shirley Lee Jenkins on March 31, 1945 in Page County, Virginia. He was born on February 23, 1926 at Stanley, Page County, Virginia. He died on July 19, 1996 in the University of Virginia Medical Center at Charlottesville, Albemarle County, Virginia and was buried in the Evergreen Memory Gardens Cemetery at Luray, Page County, Virginia. His father was Jacob Russell Jenkins of Page County, Virginia. His mother was Alma Cecil Hitt of Page County, Virginia.

William[6] and Shirley had four children: Patsy Ann[7] and three others whose names are not known.

4. William Tazewell[5] Dovel

born on March 8, 1866 at East Liberty, Page County, Virginia. He died sometime after 1930 [when he last appeared on the U. S. Census], age 64, in Page County, Virginia. He married Leah Hilary Catherine[5] [also found as Jean Hillary] Housden [sister of Cora[5] who married Charles Benton[5] Dovel] on January 26, 1892 in Page County, Virginia. She was born in 1874 in Page County, Virginia. She died in 1920 in Page County, Virginia. Her father was Perry H.[4] [Benjamin Dovel[3], Judith[2] {of Culpeper County, Virginia {{Note: John Dovel (ancestry unknown) was his natural father; however, Benjamin[3] took his mother's Housden surname}}, Benjamin[1] {of Lambeth, London, England}, William[1a] {of Bigglewade, Bedfordshire, England}] Housden of Honeyville, Page County, Virginia. Her mother was Mary Catherine [Matthew {of Hawksbill, Shenandoah County, Virginia}, Levi, Matthew] Lucas of Page County, Virginia. William[5] and Leah Hilary[5] had eight children: Maggie L.[6], Lena G.[6], Carl Sylvester[6], Minnie Mae[6], Elmer L.[6], Minnie I.[6], Myrtle V.[6] and Russell William[6].

5. Hubert Lee[5] Dovel
born on March 24, 1871 at Alma, Page County, Virginia. He died on December 30, 1849 at Mahaska, Washington County, Kansas. He married Nancy Ellen Sheldon on September 22, 1897, probably in Republic County, Kansas. She was born on November 23, 1879 in Iowa. She died on February 24, 1960 at Mahaska, Washington County, Kansas. Her father was Seth [Elisha] Sheldon of Vermont. Her mother was Mary Jane Brown of New York. Hubert[5] and Nancy had five children:

a. Lena Jane[6] Dovel
born in June 1898 in Nebraska. She died in October 1972 in Washington County, Kansas. She married Raymond A.[3] Smith sometime before 1917. He was born on June 10, 1896 in Kansas. He died on February 18, 1985 at Peabody, Marion County, Kansas. His father was John T.[2] [John B.[1] {of Mechlenberg, Germany}] Smith of Kansas. His mother was Margaret [George C. {of Ross Corners, Gregsville, Livingston County, New York}] Ferguson of Kansas. Lena[6] and Raymond[3] had six children: Alfred LeRoy[4], Arlene May[4], Clyde Dean[4], Delbert Leon[4], John Lee[4] and Harold Ray[4].

b. Henry Alden[6] Dovel
   born on March 12, 1908 in Kansas He died at birth on March 12, 1908 in Kansas.

c. William Lee[6] "Willie" Dovel
   born on June 21, 1909 in Kansas. He died on November 15, 1976 at Fairbury, Jefferson County, Nebraska. He married Mildred E. Richardson sometime before 1930, probably in Washington County, Kansas. She was born on June 23, 1911 in Kansas. She died on May 4, 1984 at Omaha, Douglas County, Nebraska. Her father was Daniel E. [Daniel S., John David] Richardson of Marion, Pike County, Indiana. Her mother was Grace Elizabeth[3] [John George[2] {of Savannah, Andrew County, Missouri}, John George[1] {of Guttels-Kreis, Germany}] Wolf of Polk, Atchison County, Missouri. William[6] and Mildred had a child: name unknown.

d. Essie Marie[6] Dovel
   born on February 10, 1911 in Kansas. She died on July 18, 1913 in Kansas.

The Life and Times of
William[3] Dovel

PATERNAL ANCESTRY: [DOVEL: David S.[2], Jr., David S.[1] {of England}]

MATERNAL ANCESTRY: [SHORT: Keziah, Samuel]

WILLIAM[3] was born on October 19, 1793 at Alma, Rockingham County, Virginia. He died on December 7, 1860 at East Liberty, Page County, Virginia. His father was David S.[2] Dovel, Jr. of Alma, Rockingham County, Virginia. His mother was Keziah Short of Virginia.

WILLIAM[3] married Christiana[4] Long circa 1821 in Virginia. She was born on April 11, 1801 in Shenandoah County, Virginia. She died on September 30, 1885 at Ingham, Page County, Virginia. Her father was Mathias[3] [Heinrick Emanual[2] {of Germany}, Philip[1] {of Alsace, Rhine River, Germany and later of Fort Long, Page County, Virginia}] Long of Shenandoah County, Virginia. Her mother was Mary[3] [John[2], Henry[1] {of Zurich, Switzerland}, Ulrich[1a], Matthias[2a] {of Wilcox, Wiltshire, England}] Heistand of Rockingham County, Virginia.

WILLIAM[3]'s death record shows that he was living at East Liberty, Summersville, age 67 years, 1 month, 10 days, a farmer and that he died of cold and paralysis.

WILLIAM[3]'s will was recorded in the Page County, Virginia Will Book H-138 and reads as follows:

> Wife, Christena to have of the farm I now live on also my black man named Joseph & my black girl named July, also one horse, which is a bay horse named Bill, 2 of my milch cows & 1 bedstead & bedding & of my personal property.
>
> Son, George W. Dovel - $1,000.00 which I have already paid for him in the purchase of his land, also the half of a piece of mountain land commencing at the old county line, Adam Dovel's corner to the top of the mountain in the County line to the leading ridge, then down that ridge, to a path a corner I have made for my son, Peter to a line formerly Joel Graves line to a corner I have made for my son, William V. Dovel to the beginning, the boundary to be divided between him & my son, St. Clair Dovel.
>
> George W. Dovel is to pay my daughter, Charity $200.00.

Son, St. Clair Dovel - the land I purchased of Cherubim Harshman. St. Clair Dovel to pay my daughter, Charity $200.00.

Son, Daniel Dovel - my mountain farm that is now in his possession. Son, John D. M. Dovel – 2 land warrants both amounting to 160 acres which he has already received. & also $100.00.

Daughter, Charity, $400.00, one bureau, two bedstead & bedding besides blankets & quilts & 1 chest all of which is owned by her, also 2 milch cows & $100.00.

Son, Peter Dovel - my interest in the lot land owned by me & my brother, Daniel Dovel undivided known as the wattery Branch & my interest being of said lot, also a piece of mountain land joining Daniel Kite, bordering Reuben Lucas.

Daughter, Martha during her lifetime - One room of my present house, 2 bedsteads & bedding.

Sons, William Dovel & Noah Dovel - the farm I now reside on to have full possession after the death of my wife.

William Dovel

Executors – Sons, Daniel Dovel
              & Noah Dovel

Witnesses – Wm. M. Dorraugh,
            David M. Dovel

Written - 16 Sep 1858 - Page Co., Va.

Recorded - 24 Dec 1860

[EDITOR'S NOTE: Regarding the land in the will, a note from a descendant named Garland Dovel that was posted on *Ancestry.com* says ". . . where they are talking about the old county line . . . and land of Adam Dovel. I own that land now, it is part of Dovel Mountain. The county line is known as the Lord Fairfax line. It was the property boundary given to Lord Fairfax by the English. There was a marker there, which would have been before the American Revolution. My father and the neighbor gave the marker to the National Park Service, and they still have it, I suppose.]

The Children of
William³ Dovel
and Christiana⁴ Long

1. Martha⁴ Dovel

born on October 16, 1822, either in Page or Rockingham County, Virginia. She died on November 30, 1898 in Page County, Virginia. [Editor's Note: She was listed on the 1850 U. S. Census as "Deaf and Dumb"].

2. St. Clair⁴ Dovel

born on March 12, 1823, either in Page or Rockingham County, Virginia. He died on May 15, 1911 at Rose Creek, Republic County, Kansas. He married Catherine Ann (Unknown) on June 30, 1850 in Page County, Virginia. She was born circa 1827 in Virginia. She died sometime after 1910 [when she last appears on the U. S. Census] at Rose Creek, Republic County, Kansas. The name of her father and mother is not known. St. Clair⁴ and Catherine had ten children:

a. Benjamin Franklin⁵ Dovel

born circa 1850/1851 in Page County, Virginia. His date and place of death is not known. He married Susan⁵ Koontz on February 27, 1872 in

Page County, Virginia. She was born circa 1853 in Page County, Virginia. Her date and place of death is not known. Her father was John J.[4] [Isaac Newton[3] {of Frederick County, Virginia}, John[2], John Annalis[1] {of Niederndorf, Germany}, Joseph[1a], Johannas[2a] {Cuntz}, Gothard[3a], Johannas[4a] {born circa 1572 in Germany}]] Koontz of Shenandoah County, Virginia. Her mother was Mary[2] [George[1] {of Germany}] Bungerman of Rockingham County, Virginia. Benjamin[5] and Susan[5] had a child: Otis Bland[6].

b. Stephen A. Douglas[5] Dovel

born on September 3, 1852 at Alma, Page County, Virginia. He died, age 17, on July 13, 1870 in Page County, Virginia.

c. Rebecca A.[5] Dovel

born on December 28, 1855 in Page County, Virginia [she was born deaf and dumb]. She died on October 31, 1937 at Cleveland, Liberty County, Texas. She married Christopher[1] Rennan in 1882 in Republic County, Kansas. He was born in May 1851 in Germany. He died on January 1, 1911 in Republic County, Kansas. The name of his father and mother is not known. Rebecca[5] and Christopher[1] had two children: Frederick[2] and Victoria[2].

d. William Preston[5] Dovel

born on March 12, 1856 at Alma, Page County, Virginia [he was born deaf and dumb]. He died on June 15, 1935, probably at Munden, Republic County, Kansas. He married Fannie Estella Hall in 1899 at Rose Creek Township, Republic County, Kansas. She was born in March 1868 at Greencastle, Marshall County, Iowa. Her date and place of death is not known. Her father was Arthur M. Hall of Oneida County, New York. Her mother was Jane Barber of New York. William[5] and Fannie had two children: Rodney Merritt[6] and Ruth Estella[6].

e. John O.[5] Dovel

born on November 15, 1857 [another record says 1858] at Alma, Page County, Virginia. He died on November 11, 1912 in Virginia [In 1910, age 50, single, he was living at Rose Creek, Republic County, Kansas].

f. Emma Elizabeth[5] Dovel

born on February 3, 1859 at Alma, Page County, Virginia. She died on February 4, 1930 at Muden, Republic County, Kansas. She married Nathaniel J. Sellers. Their date and place of marriage is not known. He was born in August

1860. His place of birth is not known. He died on October 2, 1938 in Kansas. The name of his father and mother is not known. Emma[5] and Nathaniel had a child: Elmer Taylor.

g. Annie Florence[5] Dovel

born on September 1, 1861 at Alma, Page County, Virginia. She died, age 2, in 1863 at Alma, Page County, Virginia.

h. Casper W.[5] Dovel

born circa 1866 at Alma, Page County, Virginia. His date and place of death is not known.

i. Mary Susan[5] Dovel

born on August 12, 1867 at Alma, Page County, Virginia. She died on February 23, 1934. Her place of death is not known. She married Ira W. Winterhalter.

h. Joseph Lee[5] Dovel

born on February 13, 1868 at Alma, Page County, Virginia. He died, age 17, presumably in Page County, Virginia.

3. Daniel L.[4] Dovel

born on June 5, 1827, either in Page or Rockingham County, Virginia. He died on November 4, 1886 at Honeyville, Page County, Virginia and was buried there in the William[3] Dovel Family Graveyard. He married Elizabeth Cannuut [afa Knupp] sometime before 1863 [when their first child was born] in Page County, Virginia. She was born on October 8, 1827 in Caroline County, Virginia. She died on April 28 [another researcher says April 23], 1908 in Page County, Virginia and was buried there in the William[3] Dovel Family Graveyard. The name of her father and mother is not known. Daniel[4] served during the United States Civil War in Company C, 10th Virginia Infantry from April 10, 1862 through 1865. Daniel[4] and Elizabeth had three children:

a. Casper Webster[5] Dovel

born on June 24, 1863 in Page County, Virginia. He died on December 29, 1931 at Stratford, Sherman County, Texas and was buried there in the Stratford Cemetery. He married Emma Florence Alger on January 15, 1885 in Page County, Virginia. She was born on March 20, 1862 in Page County, Virginia. She died on February 18, 1937 at Stratford, Sherman County, Texas and was buried there in the Stratford Cemetery. Her father was Andrew

Jackson [Asa] Alger of Page County, Virginia. Her mother was Mary Catherine [John {of Shenandoah County, Virginia}] Housden of Page County, Virginia. Casper[5] and Emma had eleven children: Myrtle Palma[6], Sattie Clyde[6], Millard Ernest[6], Leona C.[6], Lora Arvette[6], Vera May[6], Bernard Earl[6], Dewey Lee[6], Edna May[6], Lloyd Nelson[6] and Atlee L.[6].

b. Rosser [afa Russell] Dekalb[5] Dovel

born on June 18, 1867 in Page County, Virginia. His date and place of death is not known. He married Delilah Jane[7] Comer on December 12, 1889 in Page County, Virginia. She was born in July 1875 in Page County, Virginia. Her date and place of death is not known. Her father was Andrew Jackson[6] [John[5] {of Shenandoah County, Virginia}, Isaac[4], Michael[3], Michael[2], Christopher[1] {Gomer of Germany and later of Pennsylvania}] Comer of Page County, Virginia. Her mother was Lydia A. Catherine[6] [Andrew J.[5], John[4], Isaac[3] {of Hawksbill Creek, Page County, Virginia}, Michael[2], Michael[1] {Gaumer of Ittingen, Wertenburg Province, Germany}, Johann Christopher Hance[1a] {of Adelshofen, Baden Province, Germany}, Johann Lorenz[2a], Johann Dietrich[3a] {of Stuttguart, Germany}] Kite of Page County, Virginia. Rosser[5] and Delilah[7] had nine children: Lynn[6],

Ernest Keyser[6], Mamie Rebecca[6], Cecil A.[6], Ada I.[6], Ezra Murry[6], Vada May[6], Elmer Rosser[6] and Elizabeth Delilah[6].

c. Ida Elizabeth[5] Dovel

born on April 30, 1871 at Rileyville, Page County, Virginia. She died on December 23, 1945 in the Rockingham Memorial Hospital at Harrisonburg, Rockingham County, Virginia and was buried in the Leaks Chapel Cemetery in Page County, Virginia. She married Adam B. Alger on March 31, 1898 in Page County, Virginia. He was born on January 1, 1878 near Stanley, Page County, Virginia. He died on November 6, 1919 at home between Oak Hill and Rileyville, Page County, Virginia and was buried there in the Leaks Chapel Cemetery. His father was Andrew Jackson [Asa] Alger of Page County, Virginia. His mother was Mary Catherine [John {of Shenandoah County, Virginia}] Housden of Page County, Virginia. Elizabeth[5] and Adam had five children: Carson Ray, Carl Milbourne, Lloyd H., Floyd L. and (child).

4. George Washington[4] Dovel

born circa 1827 at Alma, Page County, Virginia. His date of death at Howe, Nemaha County,

Nebraska is not known. George[4] married Ann Elizabeth[5] Ruffner on November 30, 1848 in Page County, Virginia. She was born on February 14, 1831 at Alma, Page County, Virginia. She died on April 19, 1878 at Howe, Nemaha County, Nebraska. Her father was Mark[4] [Jonas[3] {of Shenandoah County, Virginia}, Peter[2], Peter[1] {of Kinddom of Hanover, Germany}, Jakob[1a] {of Maienfield, Germany}, Burhart[2a], Georg[3a], Hans[4a], Georg[5a], Peter[6a] {born circa 1513}] Ruffner of Page County, Virginia. Her mother was Lydia Biedler of Page County, Virginia. George[4] and Ann[5] had seven children:

a. Robert Milton[5] Dovel

born in November 1849 at Ingham, Page County, Virginia. He died on December 27, 1913 at Crimora, Augusta County, Nebraska. He married, first, Eliza Ellen Lucas on February 25, 1880 in Page County, Virginia. She was born on June 18, 1857 near Summersville, Page County, Virginia. She died of haemorrhage of the brain on November 24, 1882 at Honeyville, Page County, Virginia. Her father was William [Simeon {of Shenandoah County, Virginia}, Matthew] Lucas of Virginia. Her mother was Rebecca [Henry] Fowler of Page County, Virginia. Robert[5] and Eliza had a child: Bessie[6].

Robert[5] married, second, Martha Lee "Mattie" Lucas on December 6, 1892 in Page County, Virginia. She was born in June 1863 in Page County, Virginia. Her date and place of death is not known. Her father was William [Simeon {of Shenandoah County, Virginia}, Matthew] Lucas of Virginia. Her mother was Rebecca [Henry] Fowler of Page County, Virginia. Robert[5] and Martha had two children: William H.[6] and Robert Lloyd[6].

b. Thomas J.[5] Dovel

born in 1852 at Ingham, Page County, Virginia. His date and place of death is not known.

c. David C.[5] Dovel

born on July 3, 1853 at Ingham, Page County, Virginia. He died on October 29, 1929 at Narka, Republic County, Kansas. He married Mary W.[2] Schantz sometime before July 1882 [when their first child was born]. She was born on September 5, 1863 in Missouri. She died, age 76, on February 7, 1940, possibly in Nebraska. The name of her father and mother is not known [both were born in Germany]. David[5] and Mary[2] had three children: Henry William[6], Charles W.[6] and Clyde Clinton[6].

c. Oliver P.[5] Dovel

born on May 23, 1856 at Ingham, Page County, Virginia. He died in 1929 at Auburn, Nemaha County, Nebraska and was buried there in the Sheridan Cemetery. He married Anna I. Blount circa 1882 in Nemaha County, Nebraska. She was born in February 1861 at Auburn, Nemaha County, Nebraska [some researchers say Kentucky]. She died circa 1928 at Auburn, Nemaha County, Nebraska and was buried there in the Sheridan Cemetery. The name of her father and mother is not known [both were born in Kentucky]. Oliver[5] and Anna had a child: Elmer[6].

d. William Mark[5] Dovel

born on December 25, 1857 at Ingham, Page County, Virginia. He died on November 8, 1898 at Auburn, Nemaha County, Nebraska. He married Ellen "Ella" Johnson circa 1885 in Nemaha County, Nebraska. She was born circa 1857 at Howe, Nemaha County, Nebraska. She died on December 26, 1957 at Auburn, Nemaha County, Nebraska. The name of her father [born in Kentucky] and mother [born in Tennessee] is not known. William[5] and Ellen had four children: Mattie Myrtle[6], Herbert Wesley[6], Lulu Belle[6] and Lester[6].

e. Charles Edward[5] Dovel

born on March 30, 1860 at Ingham, Page County, Virginia. He died in 1937 in Virginia.

f. Noah W.[5] Dovel

born in 1862 at Ingham, Page County, Virginia. He died in 1895 at Howe, Nemaha County, Nebraska. He married Susan Hughes circa 1890 at Howe, Nemaha County, Nebraska. She was born circa 1858, presumably at Howe, Nemaha County, Nebraska. She died in 1939 at Kansas City, Platte County, Missouri. The name of his father and mother is not known.

g. Reuben Franklin[5] "Frank" Dovel

born in 1864 at East Liberty, Page County, Virginia. He died in 1940 at Howe, Nemaha County, Nebraska. He married Susan A.[2] Thompson circa 1889 in Nemaha County, Nebraska. She was born on August 21, 1871 at Brownville, Nemaha County, Nebraska. She died in 1947, probably at Howe, Nemaha County, Nebraska. Her father was George[1] Thompson of Susworth, Lincolnshire, England. Her mother was Mary Louise[3] [Frederick[2] {of Brownville, Nemaha County, Nebraska}, William[1] {Saddoris of Germany}, William[1a]

{Sartorius of Alsac Lorraine, Saar, Germany}]
Sedoris of Harrison County, Ohio. Reuben[5] and
Susan[2] had five children; (child)[6], Florence E.[6],
Jesse C.[6], Carl Henry[6] and Alma Aneitta[6].

5. Peter Simon[4] Dovel

born on August 8, 1821 in Shenandoah County,
Virginia. He died on February 9, 1903 in Page
County, Virginia. He married, first, Julia Ann
Jenkins on November 14, 1850 in Page County,
Virginia. She was born circa 1832 in Page County,
Virginia. She died sometime before 1860 [when
Peter[4] married second] in Page County, Virginia.
The name of her father is not known. Her mother
was Eula (Unknown) of Page County, Virginia.
Peter[4] and Julia had one child: Peter Simon[5].

Peter Simon[4] married, second, Hannah Rebecca
Houser on March 1, 1860 in Page County, Virginia.
She was born on September 5, 1838 in Page
County, Virginia. She died on June 15, 1873 at East
Liberty, Page County, Virginia. Her father was
Nicholas Houser of Pennsylvania. Her mother was
Magdalene [Phillip] Shaffer of Dry Run, Page
County, Virginia. Peter[4] and Hannah Rebecca had
three children: David Trenton[5], Charles Benton[5]
and William Tazewell[5].

Peter[4] married, third, Ann Eliza Cubbage on December 24, 1874 in Page County, Virginia. She was born circa 1837/1840 in Page County, Virginia. She died, age 56, of dropsy on September 25 [another record says the 15th], 1895 in Page County, Virginia. Her father was William [Thomas {of Page County, Virginia}, John] Cubbage of Madison County, Virginia. Her mother was Sarah[4] [Benjamin[3] {of Culpeper, Culpeper County, Virginia}, William[2], William[1] {of Whitehaven, Cumberland, England}, Thomas[1a]] Nicholson of Madison County, Virginia. Issue, if any, is not known.

6. John David [afa Daniel] Monroe[4] Dovel

born on December 16, 1830, either in Page or Rockingham County, Virginia. He died on December 7, 1923 in Page County, Virginia. He married, first, Mary Catherine[5] Anderson circa 1857, possibly in Madison County, Virginia. She was born on January 5, 1837 in Madison County, Virginia. She died of consumption on November 27, 1873 in Madison County, Virginia. Her father was Obediah[4] [Obadiah B.[3], George[2] {of Orange County, Virginia}, George[1] {of Ulster, Ireland}, Ulster[1a] {of Dowhill, Glasgow, Scotland}, John[2a] {Provost of Glasgow}, John[3a] {Lord}, John[4a] {of Dowhill, Sobcross, Scotland}, Ninian[5a], John[6a], John[7a] {born 1500}] Anderson of Madison County,

Virginia. Her mother was Eraline/Ermlina "Emma" [Ruben, John {of Culpeper, Culpeper County, Virginia}, Ambrose, William {Boughton}, Joshua {of Essex County, Virginia] Booton of Madison County, Virginia. John[4] and Mary[5] had one child:

a. Milton Obediah[5] Dovel

born on March 17, 1868 near Grove Hill, Page County, Virginia. He died on March 16, 1923 at Orlando, Orange County, Florida. He married Alma Chapman in 1910 at Narka, Republic County, Kansas. She was born in May 1872 at Narka, Republic County, Kansas. She died on April 5, 1964 at Orlando, Orange County, Florida. The name of her father and mother is not known. Milton[5] and Alma had two children: Mildred C.[6] and Junius Elmore[6].

John[4] married, second, Eliza A.[5] Koontz on December 14, 1875 in Page County, Virginia. She was born in 1839 in Page County, Virginia. She died on May 10, 1921 at Albion, Republic County, Kansas. Her father was John J.[4] [Isaac Newton[3] {of Frederick County, Virginia}, John[2], John Annalis[1] {of Niederndorf, Germany), Joseph[1a], Johannes[2a] {Cantz}, Gothard[3a], Johannes[4a]] Koontz of Shenandoah County, Virginia. Her mother was Penelope

Mary[2] "Polly" [George[1] {born circa 1780}] Bungerman of Rockingham County, Virginia [other researchers say her parents are Daniel K. Koontz and Elizabeth Mauck of Page County, Virginia]. John[4] and Eliza[5] had two children:

b. Mary Blanch[5] Dovel

born on November 3, 1876 at Honeyville, Page County, Virginia. She died on September 18, 1961 at Buffalo, Dallas County, Missouri. She married Charles Franklin Thomas on February 22, 1898 at Belleville, Chautauqua County, Kansas. He was born on October 21, 1873 in Boone County, Iowa. He died on December 1, 1943 at Buffalo, Dallas County, Missouri. His father was John Henson [William H. {of Madison County, Kentucky}] Thomas of Clay County, Indiana. His mother was Rachel [Jones W., Lewis Jones {of Lexington, Fayette County, Kentucky}] Harris of Butler County, Ohio. Mary[5] and Charles had two children: Charles Edwin and Curtis Leon.

c. William Delwin[5] Dovel

born on August 13, 1898 at Newport, Page County, Virginia. He died on January 3, 1942 at Boulder, Boulder County, Colorado. He married Phrana Zarelda[6] Bever, sometime before 1906 [when their first child was born] in Republic County, Kansas. She was born on November 28, 1882 in Illinois. She died on February 9, 1970 at Boulder, Boulder County, Colorado. Her father was Simon[5] [Christian[4] {of Adams County, Ohio}, Michael[3] {of Harrison County, Kentucky}, Matthias[2] {of Harrison City, Allegheny County, Pennsylvania}, Peter[1] {of Hirschland, Germany}, Peter[1a] {Bieber}, Hans Dietrich[2a], Simon[3a] {Haber of France}, Simon[4a] {born circa 1550 in France}] Bever of Hillsboro, Fountain County, Indiana. Her mother was Melissa Jane [William {of Licking County, Ohio}, Joseph B. {of Pennsylvania}] Peters of Cain, Fountain County, Indiana. William[5] and Phrana[6] had five children: Myles D.[6], Floyd Milton[6], (child)[6], (child)[6] and Wilma Dorothy[6].

7. Charity[4] [afa Elizabeth] Dovel

born circa 1834, either in Page or Rockingham County, Virginia. Her date and place of death is not known. She married Joseph[4] Spitler on December 24, 1861 in Page County, Virginia. He was born on December 5, 1827 in Shenandoah County, Virginia. He died of pleuro-pneumonia on January 13, 1885 at Mill Creek, Page County, Virginia and was buried there in the Spitler Family Cemetery. His father was Isaac[3] [Abraham L.[2] {of Augusta County, Virginia}, John[1] {of Switzerland}]

Spitler of Shenandoah County, Virginia. His mother was Esther[3] [George[2] {of Orange County, Virginia}, Jacob[1] {of Wallisellin, Zurich, Switzerland}, Jacob[1a] {of Klotten, Zurich, Switzerland}, Rudolf[2a]] Rothgeb of Shenandoah County, Virginia. Issue, if any, is not known.

Joseph[4] is recorded as marrying, second, an (Unknown) Roller, who was born on March 14, 1843 in Virginia and marrying, third, an Elizabeth (Unknown), who was born in 1828 in Virginia [Editor's Note: Nothing else is known of these marriages].

8. William A.[4] Dovel

born on May 2, 1840, either in Page or Rockingham County, Virginia. He died on August 11, 1898 in Page County, Virginia and was buried there in the William Dovel Cemetery. He married Rebecca Knupp on March 16, 1879 in Page County, Virginia. Rebecca was born on April 18, 1831 in Page County, Virginia. She died on March 10, 1929 in Page County, Virginia and was buried there in the William Dovel Cemetery. Her father was William [Abraham, Peter] Knupp of Rockingham County, Virginia. Her mother was Anna Frank of Rockingham County, Virginia. William[4] was a boatman in the flat boats that carried iron ore and other goods downstream on the South Fork of the Shenandoah River to Harper's Ferry. William[4] and Rebecca had five children:

a. Annie Virginia[5] Dovel

born in January 1877 in Page County, Virginia. She died in 1959 in Virginia. She married Samuel Tildon Stepp on September 20, 1904 in Page County, Virginia. He was born on September 10, 1876 at Shenandoah, Page County, Virginia. He died in 1966 in Virginia. His father was David Stepp of Page County, Virginia. His mother was Mary Catherine [David {of Caroline County, Virginia}, John M.] Keyser of Page County, Virginia. Annie[5] and Samuel had two children: Lucille Virginia and Tessie M.

b. Charles Edward[5] Dovel

born on May 29, 1879 in Page County, Virginia. He died on January 31, 1947 in Page County, Virginia and was buried there in the Dovel Cemetery at Grove Hill. He married Zula Elizabeth Walters on April 6, 1927 in Page County, Virginia. She was born on February 16, 1907 at Shenandoah, Page County, Virginia. She died on June 5, 1955 at Shenandoah, Page County, Virginia and was buried there on June

8, 1955 in the Rest Haven Cemetery. Her father was Jacob Casper [Thomas William {of Warren County, Virginia}, Jacob] Walters of Catherine's Furnace, Page County, Virginia. Her mother was Mary Elizabeth [Jackson] Short of Page County, Virginia. Issue, if any, is not known.

c. (son)[5] Dovel

born circa 1881 in Page County, Virginia. His date and place of death is not known.

d. Mary L.[5] Dovel

born in November 1889 in Page County, Virginia. Her date and place of death is not known. She married Samuel Smith. He was born circa 1886 in Virginia.

e. Mamie Lee[5] Dovel

born in 1893 in Page County, Virginia. Her date and place of death is not known. She married Charles Marion May on October 28, 1920 in Page County, Virginia. He was born on June 7, 1882 in Page County, Virginia. His date and place of death is not known. His father was Benjamin F. [Henry] May of Page County, Virginia. His mother was Rhoda Ann Dean of Page County, Virginia. Mamie[5] and Charles had two children: Alva L. and Silva L.

8. Noah[4] Dovel

born circa 1841, either in Page or Rockingham County, Virginia. He was a Confederate soldier during the U. S. Civil War. He enlisted as a Private at age 20 on June 1, 1861. He was in Company E, Calvary Regiment of Virginia. He was killed in action on June 21, 1863 at Upperville, Fauquier County, Virginia.

The Battle of Upperville took place on June 21, 1863, the outcome being inconclusive. Major General Alfred Pleasonton commanded the Union troops; Brigadier General Wade Hampton and Brigadier General Beverly Robertson the CSA troops. Both sides had forces that added up to divisional strength. Union cavalry made a determined effort to pierce Stuart's cavalry screen. Hampton's and Robertson's brigades made a stand at Goose Creek, west of Middleburg and beat back Gregg's division. Buford's column detoured to attack the Confederate left flank near Upperville, but encountered William E. "Grumble" Jones' and John R. Chambliss' brigades, while J. I. Gregg's and Kilpatrick's brigades advanced on Upperville from the east along the Little River Turnpike. After furious mounted fighting, Stuart withdrew to take a strong defensive position in Ashby Gap, even as Confederate infantry crossed the Potomac in Maryland. As cavalry skirmishing diminished, Stuart made the fateful decision to strike east and make a circuit of the Union army as it marched toward Gettysburg. There were about 400 total casualties, including Noah[4] Dovel.

The Life and Times of
David S.² Dovel, Jr.

PATERNAL ANCESTRY: [DOVEL: David S.¹ {of England}]

MATERNAL ANCESTRY: [BLOSSER: Barbara]

DAVID S.², Jr. was born on April 15, 1768 at Alma, Rockingham County, Virginia. He died in February 1832 at Alma, Page County, Virginia. His father was David S.¹ Dovel of England. His mother was Barbara Blosser [1773-1820] of Caroline, Rockingham County, Virginia.

DAVID S.², Jr. married Keziah Short circa 1793 in Rockingham County, Virginia. She was born on August 20, 1774 in Virginia. She died sometime between 1850 and 1860 in Page County, Virginia. Her father was Samuel [Samuel, Samuel {of Rappahannock County, Virginia}, Thomas] Short of Virginia. Her mother was Hannah (Unknown).

[EDITOR'S NOTE: The area the Dovel families settled in Rockingham County, Virginia later became part of Page County; Page County was formed in 1831 from sections of Rockingham and Shenandoah Counties]

The Children of
David S.[2] Dovel, Jr.
and Keziah Short

1. William[3] Dovel

born on October 19, 1793 at Alma, Rockingham County, Virginia. He died of a cold and paralysis on December 7, 1860 at East Liberty, Page County, Virginia. He married Christiana[4] Long circa 1821 in Virginia. She was born on April 11, 1801 in Shenandoah County, Virginia. She died on September 30, 1885 at Ingham, Page County, Virginia. Her father was Mathias[3] [Heinrick Emanual[2] {of Germany}, Philip[1] {of Alsace, Rhine River, Germany and later of Fort Long, Page County, Virginia}] Long of Shenandoah County, Virginia. Her mother was Mary [John] Heistand of Rockingham County, Virginia. William[3] and Christiana[4] had eight children: Martha[4], St. Clair[4], Daniel[4], George W.[4], Peter Simon[4], John David[4], Charity[4] and Noah[4].

2. John W.[3] Dovel

born on October 19, 1793 at Alma, Page County, Virginia. He died on October 17, 1864 in Rockingham County, Virginia. He married Sarah "Sallie" Shuler [the sister of George, who married Talitha[3] Dovel, and of Eva, who married Daniel D.[3] Dovel] on December 21, 1819 in Page County, Virginia.

Sarah was born circa 1799 in Virginia. She died on September 7, 1867 at Stone Wall, Rockingham County, Virginia. Her father was John [John Matthias {of Pennsylvania}] Shuler of Rockingham County, Virginia. His mother was Mary Magdalena[2] [Valentine[1] {of Rumpenheim, Hesse, Germany}, Valentine[1a], Stephen[2a] {Kayser}, Valentine[3a], Johhann[4a] {born circa 1575}] Kiser of Cumru Township, Berks County, Pennsylvania. John[3] and Sarah had eight children:

a. Diana[4] Dovel

born on May 27, 1824 in Rockingham County, Virginia. She died on December 25, 1899 in Virginia. She married Noah Martz on August 25, 1841 in Virginia. He was born on April 13, 1820. He died on November 14, 1888. The name of his father and mother is not known. Diana[4] and Noah had eight children: John William, David Richard, Charles Miffin, Sarah Catherine, Francis Marion, Caroline Virginia, Turner Ashby and Josephine E.

b. Virginia Jane[4] Dovel

born circa 1826 in Rockingham County, Virginia. Her date and place of death is not known. She married Adam Long on March 23, 1849 in Rockingham County, Virginia. He was born circa 1824 in Virginia. His date and place of death is not known. The name of his father and mother is not known. Virginia[4] and Adam had two children: Joseph F. and Sarah.

c. James T.[4] Dovel

born on November 19, 1827 in Rockingham County, Virginia. He died on April 24, 1904. He married Sarah (Unknown).

d. Charles W.[4] Dovel

born on March 11, 1832 in Rockingham County, Virginia. He died on May 19, 1897 in the home of P. H. Dovel at Elkton, Rockingham County, Virginia. He married Talitha Jane[4] Dovel on March 16, 1854 in Rockingham County, Virginia. She was born on March 28, 1835 in Page County, Virginia. She died in February 1921 at Elkton, Rockingham County, Virginia. Her father was Adam Beauregard[3] [George[2] {of Shenandoah County, Virginia}, David S.[1] {of England}] Dovel of Page County, Virginia. Her mother was Dianna [George] Shuler of Page County, Virginia. Charles[4] and Talitha[4] had nine children: Dianna Ann[5], Fidilia[5], John Adam[5], Mary[5], Sarah[5], Charles Clinton[5], Ashby[5], Susan R.[5] and David R.[5].

e. Jackson[4] Dovel

born circa 1834/1836 in Rockingham County, Virginia. His date and place of death is not known [he probably died young].

f. Daniel D.[4] Dovel

born circa 1838 in Rockingham County, Virginia. He died in 1901 in Page County, Virginia. He married Mary Jane Barlow sometime before 1874 [when their first child was born], presumably in Page County, Virginia. She was born circa 1838 in Virginia. Her date and place of death is not known. The name of her father and mother is not known. Daniel[4] and Mary Jane had two children: Sarah E.[5] and Laurie Victoria[5].

g. Cinderella[4] Dovel

born circa 1841 in Rockingham County, Virginia. She died on December 2, 1872 at Elkton, Rockingham County, Virginia. She married Lucius Bonaparte[4] Dovel in 1867 in Rockingham County, Virginia. He was born in February 1838 at Mt. Crawford, Rockingham County, Virginia. He died in 1907 at Harrisonburg, Rockingham County, Virginia. His father was Tandy E.[3] [Daniel[2], David S.[1] {of England}]

Dovel of Mt. Crawford, Rockingham County, Virginia. His mother was Catherine Lamb of Virginia. Cinderella[4] and Lucius[4] had four children: Calvin Bird[5], Patrick Henry[5], Laura F.[5] and Eugene Walter[5].

Lucius[4] married, second, Dianna Ann[5] Dovel on June 7, 1877 in Rockingham County, Virginia. She was born on November 12, 1857 in Rockingham County, Virginia. She died on February 25, 1931 in Rockingham County, Virginia. Her father was Charles W.[4] [John W.[3], David[2], Daniel S.[1] {of England}]] Dovel of Rockingham County, Virginia. Her mother was Talitha Jane[4] [Adam Beauregard[3], George[2], David S.[1] {of England}]] Dovel of Page County, Virginia. Lucius[4] and Dianna[5] had three children: Dorothea Ann[5] "Dorothy," Celestor[5] and Cora Belle[5].

h. Mary A.[4] Dovel

born on December 30, 1842 in Rockingham County, Virginia. She died on March 17, 1913, possibly in Fauquier County, Virginia. She married Tandy E.[4] Dovel, Jr. sometime before 1864 [when their first child was born], presumably in Rockingham County, Virginia. He was born on September 17, 1842 at Mt.

Crawford, Rockingham County, Virginia. He died on January 12, 1909 in Fauquier County, Virginia. His father was Tandy E.[3] [Daniel[2], David S.[1] {of England}] Dovel of Mt. Crawford, Rockingham County, Virginia. His mother was Catherine Lamb of Virginia. Mary[4] and Tandy[4] had seven children: Fitzhugh L.[5], William H.[5], Richard W.[5], George E.[5], Tandy[5], Charles Wesley[5] and Sarah C.[5].

3. Talitha B.[3] Dovel
   born on September 19, 1795 at Alma, Rockingham County, Virginia. She died on June 18, 1857 in Page County, Virginia. She married George Shuler [the brother of Eva "Elva" Shuler, who married Daniel D.[3] Dovel, and Sarah, who married John W.[3] Dovel] on June 8, 1814 in Rockingham County, Virginia. He was born on December 25, 1794 in Rockingham County, Virginia. He died on April 28, 1873 in Page County, Virginia. His father was John [John Matthias {of Pennsylvania}] Shuler of Rockingham County, Virginia. His mother was Mary Magdalena[2] [Valentine[1] {of Rumpenheim, Hesse, Germany}, Valentine[1a], Stephen[2a] {Kayser}, Valentine[3a], Johhann[4a] {born circa 1575] Kiser of Cumru Township, Berks County, Pennsylvania. Talitha[3] and George had eight children:

a. John Shuler

born on August 18, 1815 in Rockingham County, Virginia. He died on March 24, 1908 Page County, Virginia. He married Mary Ann Kite on November 22, 1838 in Page County, Virginia. She was born on November 18, 1820 in Shenandoah County, Virginia. She died on July 12, 1897 in Page County, Virginia. Her father was John Kite of Shenandoah County, Virginia. Her mother was Delia Armentrout of Shenandoah County, Virginia. John and Mary Ann had ten children: Harriet E., Michael, Emily Jane, Isaac, Amanda Virginia, John W., George Thomas, James Jackson, Mary Ann and Sallie Belle.

b. Dianne "Diana" Shuler

born on October 17. 1819 in Rockingham County, Virginia. Her date and place of death is not known. She married Adam Dovel on September 30, 1835 in Page County, Virginia. He was born circa 1815 in Page County, Virginia.

c. Noah W. Shuler

born on September 20, 1821 in Rockingham County, Virginia. He died sometime after 1900 [when he last appears on the U. S. Census] in Rockingham County, Virginia. He married Keziah Dovel in 1844, presumably in Rockingham County, Virginia. She was born in June 1825 in Virginia. She died sometime after 1900 [when she last appears on the U. S. Census] in Rockingham County, Virginia. Her father was Daniel D. Dovel of Virginia. Her mother was Eve [John, John Matthias {of Pennsylvania}, Mathias {of Augusta County, Virginia}] Shuler of Rockingham County, Virginia. Noah and Keziah had fourteen children: (child), Elizabeth, Daniel P., Joseph R., John W., (child), Fidelia/Phedilia, Sarah, Peter N., George W., (child), Benjamin Franklin, (child) and Chancellor Hour.

d. Elizabeth Ann Shuler

born on October 29, 1824 in Virginia. She died circa 1846 in Virginia. She married John D.[5] Aylshire [afa Aleshire] on September 12, 1842 in Page County, Virginia. He was born on March 15, 1821 in Shenandoah County, Virginia. He died, age 40, on January 16, 1862 in Page County, Virginia. His father was Joseph A.[4] [Joseph A.[3], Christian Lion[2] {Eischeidt}, Johann Conrad[1] {of Neiderhonnefelf, Neuwied, Rheinland-Pfaltz, Germany}, Jeremias[1a], Wilhelm[2a]] Aleshire of Shenandoah County, Virginia. His

161

mother was Sarah "Sally" [John {of Frederick County, Virginia}, John, John] Koontz of Page County, Virginia. Issue, if any, is not known.

John[5] married, second, Sarah Jane Shuler on August 28, 1856 in Page County, Virginia. She was born on May 12, 1836 in Page County, Virginia. She died on April 25, 1894 at Nickerson, Reno County, Kansas and was buried there in the Wildmead Cemetery. Her father was George [John, John Matthias {of Pennsylvania}] Shuler of Rockingham County, Virginia. Her mother was Talitha B.[3] [David S.[2] {of Alma, Page County, Virginia}, David S.[1] {of England}] Dovel of Rockingham County, Virginia. John[5] and Sarah had two children: Sarah Elizabeth[6] and Rebecca A.[6]

e. George Washington Shuler

born on January 26, 1830 in Caroline County, Virginia. He died May 17, 1918 in Page County, Virginia and was buried there in the Shuler Family Graveyard at Shenandoah. He married Catherine Kite on December 24, 1849 in Page County, Virginia. She was born on September 9, 1830 in Caroline County, Virginia. She died on December 17, 1906 in Page County, Virginia and was buried there in the Shuler Family

Graveyard at Shenandoah. The name of her father and mother is not known. George and Catherine had nine children: David H., Hiram Jackson, Joseph Taswell, Viola V., Franklin Lee, George Amos, Bertie L., Elizabeth A. and Catherine.

f. Andrew Jackson Shuler

born on February 2, 1831 in Virginia. He died on March 13, 1911 in Virginia. He married Julia Ann[4] Koontz on November 15, 1850 in Page County, Virginia. She was born on February 15, 1836 in Page County, Virginia. She died on April 29, 1873 in Page County, Virginia. Her father was Isaac Newton[3] [John[2], John Annalis[1] {of Niederndorf, Germany}, Josheph[1a], Johannes[2a] {Cantz}, Gothard[3a], Johannes[4a]] Koontz of Frederick County, Virginia. Her mother was Ann [George] Keyser of Page County, Virginia. Andrew and Julia[4] had nine children: Isaac Ferdinand, William Harrison, Noah Washington, George W., Charles Trenton, David Jackson, Anna Belle, John Newton and Emma Jane.

Andrew married, second, Alcinda N. Brown circa 1874 in Page County, Virginia. She was born on November 14, 1836 in Page County,

Virginia. She died on August 4, 1887 in Page County, Virginia and was buried there in the Koontz-Shuler Family Cemetery at Alma. The name of her father and mother is not known. Issue, if any, is not known.

Andrew married, third, Emma E. Buracker on February 20, 1900 in Page County, Virginia. She was born on February 21, 1852 at Cedar Point, Page County, Iowa. She died on October 18, 1906 in Page County, Virginia and was buried there in the Buracker Family Graveyard at Big Spring Farm, near Rileyville. The name of her father and mother is not known. There was no issue.

g. William D. Shuler

born on June 23, 1833 in Page County, Virginia. He died on December 27, 1924 in Reno County, Kansas and was buried there in the Mitchell Cemetery at Hutchinson. He married Sarah Koontz on August 9, 1855 in Page County, Virginia. She was born on August 28, 1839 in Page County, Virginia. She died on October 19, 1896 in Reno County, Kansas and was buried there in the Mitchell Cemetery at Hutchinson. Her father was David Koontz of Page County, Virginia. Her mother was Catherine Foltz of

Page County, Virginia. William and Sarah had five children: Phillip Preston, Jacob O., William T. B. A. Lee, Martin B. and Walter Amos.

h. Sarah Jane Shuler

born on May 12, 1836 in Page County, Virginia. She died on April 25, 1894 at Nickerson, Reno County, Kansas and was buried there in the Wildmead Cemetery. She married John D. Aylshire [afa Aleshire] on August 28, 1856 in Page County, Virginia. He was born on March 15, 1821 in Page County, Virginia. He was killed sometime before July 1866 in a battle during the U. S. Civil war. The name of his father and mother is not known.

Sarah Jane married, second, James Edward Morris on July 12, 1866 in Page County, Virginia. He was born on May 31, 1830 at Leaksville, Page County, Virginia. He died, age 84 years, 4 months, 5 days, on October 6, 1914 at Nickerson, Reno County, Kansas and was buried there in the Wildmead Cemetery. The name of his father and mother is not known. James fought with the Confederacy in the U. S. Civil War. Sara and James had five children: George W., Mattie, A. J., Anna and T. A.

George married, second, Eva Catherine[4] Kiser on July 8, 1860 in Page County, Virginia. She was born on September 11, 1801 in Rockingham County, Virginia. She died on May 22, 1886 in Page County, Virginia. Her father was John[3] [Michael[2] {of Pennsylvania}, Charles[1] "Carl" {Keyser of the Duchy of Wirtemburg, Germany}]] Kiser of Rockingham County, Virginia. Her mother was Margaret "Peggy" [George] Null of Rockingham County, Virginia. There was no issue.

Eva[4] had married, first, John "Boggy" Kite on April 3, 1819 in Rockingham County, Virginia. He was born on December 25, 1794 in Rockingham County, Virginia [another record says January 10, 1787 at Grove Hill, Shenandoah County, Virginia]. He died on April 1, 1855 at Grove Hill, Shenandoah County, Virginia. His father was John [John Windel, James] Kite of Rockingham County, Virginia. His mother was Christina Miller of Rockingham County, Virginia. Eva[4] and John had fifteen children: Martin Van Buren, Alfred M., A. F., Benjamin, Mary Ann, Reuben, Anna, Oliver Henry, Catherine, James J., Margaret, John W., Jacob B., George Washington and John D.

4. Daniel D.[3] Dovel
   born on August 16, 1800 at Alma, Rockingham County, Virginia. He died on July 30, 1867 in Page

County, Virginia and was buried in the East Point Cemetery at Elkton, Rockingham County, Virginia. He married Eva "Elva" Shuler [the sister of George, who married Talitha[3] Dovel, and Sarah, who married John Walter[3] Dovel] on December 20, 1819 [another record says on the 21st] in Rockingham County, Virginia. She was born circa 1799/1803 in Virginia. She died on September 7, 1867 in Rockingham County, Virginia and was buried there in the East Point Cemetery at Elkton. Her father was John [John Matthias {of Pennsylvania}] Shuler of Rockingham County, Virginia. Her mother was Mary Magdalena[2] [Valentine[1] {of Rumpenheim, Hesse, Germany}, Valentine[1a], Stephen[2a] {Kayser}, Valentine[3a], Johann[4a] {born circa 1575}] Kiser of Cumru Township, Berks County, Pennsylvania. Daniel[3] and Eva had fourteen children:

a. David[4] Dovel

born on November 9, 1821 at Alma, Rockingham County, Virginia. He died, age 2 months, 7 days, on January 15, 1822 at Alma, Rockinham County, Virginia.

b. Elizabeth[4] Dovel

born on January 31, 1823 at Alma, Rockingham County, Virginia. She died, age 29, on July 4,

1852 at Alma, Rockingham County, Virginia. She married Jeremiah Petefish on August 20, 1841. His date and place of birth and death is not known. The name of his father and mother is not known. Issue, if any, is not known.

c. Keziah[4] Dovel

born on July 11, 1825 at Alma, Rockingham County, Virginia. She died, age 78, on February 3, 1904 in Rockingham County, Virginia. She married Noah W. Shuler circa 1843 in Rockingham County, Virginia. He was born on September 1821 in Rockingham County, Virginia. He died on December 4, 1909 in Rockingham County, Virginia. His father was George [John, John Matthias {of Pennsylvania}] of Rockingham County, Virginia. His mother was Talitha B.[3] [David S.[2], David S.[1] {of England}] Dovel of Alma, Rockingham County, Virginia. Keziah[4] and Noah had fourteen children: (child), Elizabeth Ann, Daniel P., Joseph R., John W., (child), Fidelia, Sarah, Peter N., George W., (child), Benjamin Franklin, (child) and Chancellor Hour.

d. Jameson Henry[4] "James" Dovel

born on November 19, 1827 at Alma, Rockingham County, Virginia. He died, age 76, on April

27, 1904. His place of death is not known. He married Eliza C. Long circa 1851 in Rockingham County, Virginia. She was born in March 1934 in Virginia. She died on October 31, 1903. Her place of death is not known. Her father was Paul [John, John Mattias {of Pennsylvania}] Long of Rockland County, Virginia. Her mother was Elizabeth Shuler of Rockingham County, Virginia. Jameson[4] and Eliza had thirteen children: Charles B.[5], Eve Angeline[5], Elizabeth F.[5], Robert D.[5], Sarah Catherine[5], Keziah[5], Rebecca J.[5], Henrietta[5], Philip G.[5], Jenetta[5], Eliza E.[5], Rose L.[5] and Josephine[5].

e. Gordianus[4] Dovel

born on May 10, 1830 at Alma, Rockingham County, Virginia. He died, age 77, on June 3, 1907 in Shenandoah County, Virginia. He married Barbara Ann Summers on November 27, 1851 in Page County, Virginia. She was born on September 25, 1835 in Virginia. She died on June 10, 1899 in Grove Hill, Madison County, Georgia. The name of her father and mother is not known. Gordianus[4] and Barbara had eight children: Hiram Jackson[5], William Henry[5], Mary Catherine[5], George Washington[5], David B.[5], Thomas Jefferson[5], Clarissa Ann[5] and Charles Ashby[5].

f. Martain⁴ Dovel

born on November 9, 1832 at Alma, Rocking-
ham County, Virginia. He died, age 6 days, on
November 15, 1832 at Alma, Rockingham
County, Virginia.

g. Talitha⁴ Dovel

born on March 16, 1834 at Alma, Rockingham
County, Virginia. She died, age 5 months, 21
days, on September 6, 1834 at Alma, Rockingham County, Virginia.

h. Andrew Jackson⁴ Dovel

born on August 31, 1825 at Alma, Rockingham
County, Virginia. His date and place of death is
not known.

i. Minerva Ann⁴ Dovel

born on July 25, 1838 at Alma, Rockingham
County, Virginia. She died, age 57, on July 3,
1896 at Alma, Rockingham County, Virginia.
She married Phillip S.⁵ Koontz on April 10, 1856
in Rockingham County, Virginia. He was born
on February 4, 1836 in Virginia. He died on
June 15, 1889 in Virginia. His father was David
B.⁴ [Isaac Newton³ {of Page County, Virginia},
John² {of Opequon, Frederick County, Virginia},

John[1] {of Germany}] Koontz of Shenandoah County, Virginia. His mother was Catherine [John Philip] Foltz of Shenandoah County, Virginia. Minerva[4] and Phillip[5] had twelve children: John D.[6], Daniel P.[6], Noah Washington[6], Mary M. L.[6], Charles P.[6], Evie C.[6], Virginia Belle[6], Cleophus Edward Lewis[6], Ida Florence[6], Cordelia Minerva Jane[6], Andrew Jackson[6] and James Granville[6].

j. Jennetta Ann[4] Dovel

born on January 17, 1841 at Alma, Rockingham County, Virginia. She died, age 81, on March 24, 1922 in Albemarle County, Virginia. She married Phillip Penelton Shifflett on December 13, 1859 in Albemarle County, Virginia. He was born on October 29, 1837 in Albemarle County, Virginia. He died on March 16, 1919 at Shenandoah, Albemarle County, Virginia. The name of his father and mother is not known. Jennetta[4] and Phillip had fourteen children: Eve Catherine, Alpharetta Susan, Mitta Lee Emaline, Jennetta Mariam, Era Ella, Alice Endora, Issac P., Lucille Mildred, William Taylor, Lycurgous Ashby, Millard Wise, Susan, Virginia and Ora A.

k. Pamlian[4] Dovel

born on May 31, 1843 at Alma, Rockingham County, Virginia. She died, age 2 years, 15 days, on June 15, 1845 at Alma, Rockingham County, Virginia.

l. Emmaline L.[4] "Emma" Dovel

born on July 15, 1846 at Alma, Rockingham County, Virginia. She died, age 75, on February 2, 1922 in Virginia. She married John W.[8] Burkett on May 16, 1865 in Rockingham County, Virginia. He was born on August 16, 1837 in Rockingham County, Virginia. He died on January 7, 1916 in Virginia. His father was William Burkhead[7] [Nehemiah[6], Edward F.[5] {Birkhead of Anne Arundel County, Maryland}, Nehemiah[4] III, Nehemiah[3] II, Nehemiah[2], Christopher[1] II {of Bristol, Gloucester County, England}, Christopher[1a] I, Christopher[2a]] of Albemarle County, Virginia. His mother was Mary A. Peyton of Virginia. Emmaline[4] and John[8] had eleven children: Mary Catherine[9], Sarah A.[9], Ida B.[9], Jenetta E.[9], Betty Ann[9], Susan J.[9], Emmaline[9] "Florence," John Edgar[9], William H.[9], Grace Folsome[9] and Minnie[9].

m. Daniel Livingston[4] Dovel

born on May 25, 1848 at Alma, Rockingham County, Virginia. His date and place of death is not known [Editor's Note: He disappears after the 1860 U. S. Census].

n. DeLafayette[4] Dovel

born on August 4, 1850 at Alma, Rockingham County, Virginia. He died, age 71, on November 24, 1921 at Corsicana, Navarro County, Texas. He married Louise Elizabeth[6] Long on January 8, 1871 in Rockingham County, Virginia. She was born on August 28, 1850 in Virginia. She died, age 64, on September 22, 1914 at Telferner, Victoria County, Texas. Her father was Layton Nicholas[5] [George Ludwig Lewis[4] {of Rockingham County, Virginia}, Phillip[3] {of Fort Long, Shenandoah County, Virginia}, Phillip[2], Paul[1] {of Germany}, Philip[1a] {of Alsac, Rhine River, Germany}, Johannes[2a] {of Ingelfingen Parish, Criesbach Kunzbach, Boden-Wurttemberg, Germany}, Conrad[3a] {Lung}, Gabel[4a] {born circa 1560}] Long of Orange County, Virginia. Her mother was Rebecca Jane[6] [Samuel[5], John[4] {of Calvert County, Maryland}, Peter[3], John[2], Bartholomew[1] {of England}] Gibson of Greene County, Virginia. DeLafayette[4] and Louise[6] had six children: Virginia May[5], Alunzo Mellons[5], Eugene Amos[5], Elizabeth Eva Jane[5], Henretia Melissa[5] and Nasissa Clementine[5].

5. Charles C.[3] Dovel
born on March 15, 1806 at Alma, Rockingham County, Virginia. He died on October 17, 1864 in Page County, Virginia. He married Elizabeth[3] Koontz on March 1, 1827 in Page County, Virginia. She was born on December 24, 1809 in Page County, Virginia. She died on January 13, 1875 in Page County, Virginia and buried there in the Shuler-Koontz Cemetery. Her father was Isaac Newton[3] [John[2], John Annalis[1] {of Niederndorf, Germany), Josheph[1a], Johannes[2a] {Cantz}, Gothard[3a], Johannes[4a]] Koontz of Frederick County, Virginia. Her mother was Susanna[2] [Johans Daniel[1] {Kublinger of Rhein-durkeim, Worms, Rheinland-Pfaltz, Germany}]] Kiblinger of Rockingham County, Virginia.

What follows is a story about the Charles C.[3] Dovel family:

How the slave woman "Old Sill" ran
the Charles C. Dovel family household

In the book entitled *The Families of Adam Beauregard Dovel* there is a small account of one Dovel family and its interaction with a well respected and, obviously, outspoken slave woman named Drucilla, or, "Old Sill."

Born in 1806, Charles C. Dovel, in 1827, married Elizabeth Koontz, the daughter of Isaac and Susanna Kiblinger Koontz, Sr. Elizabeth and her new husband immediately made their home on her father's homestead in Alma. The son and son-in-law of slave-holders (fewer than three slaves each), Charles would own only two slaves, including "Old Sill" who was born around 1820 and had been left to him in 1832 by his father's will.

According to the Dovel book, the story pertaining to "Sill" was extracted from an undated clipping from an old *Page News & Courier* and was written by Jacob R. Seekford. While small in length, it is of interest in the further understanding of how one of Page County's over 1,000 slaves that resided in the county from 1840-1860 experienced life.

Seekford began: "Only a few slave owners living in this part of the county would have taken their slaves back after the war. Many of them were glad that the slaves were set free. I knew all of the old slaves of this county and the old masters and mistresses never let one suffer when they lived near their homes. I have seen as many as six of these old slaves, men and women, around one home when these big homes would have a big dinner." However, Seekford noted, "the Koontzes, Shulers and Dovels, who lived around Alma . . . were not fitting people to have slaves in many cases because they gave the slaves more privileges than they gave their own children. I never heard one of them that ever whipped a slave and they kept them more for pets than anything else."

Seekford went on to state that one slave in the Dovel household, "Sill," struck an imposing figure at "about 225 pounds" and had been "the complete boss of the Dovel home and ran things just to suit herself . . . ," showing how much the slave woman interacted with the family. Seekford continued that she was responsible for having named all of the Dovel children, including Drucilla, whom she named after herself. Interestingly, all of the girls names closely resembled "Sill," including Priscilla and Cecilia.

When it came to disciplining the children, Seekford recalled that the children's own mother "never whipped one of them, but Old Sill laid the lash on them whenever she found it convenient." Seekford had once "heard one of the Dovel boys say that she whipped Russell Dovel with a switch when he was thirteen years old." Sill, on occasion, even found time to "get-after" her master Charles. "I have heard the late David Dovel tell about this woman putting her hands in his father's coat collar and threatening to whip him," wrote Seekford. Furthermore, to show just how much she ruled the household affairs, Seekford remembered that "She also bossed and ran" Dovel's home distillery. "She looked after the selling of brandy, in fact, she carried the key to the cellar where the liquor was kept."

Charles C. Dovel died in 1864, and, despite the emancipation and constant flow of Federal troops through Page County during the war, she did not leave the county until 1868. "She came back here [from Charles County] in 1872," wrote Seekford, "and stayed about a year and spent all of her time with the Dovel children . . . . She nursed old Daniel Koontz when he was sick and laid him out when he died." "Sill" later returned to Clarke County where she died and was buried at the Old Stone Chapel.

Charles[3] and Elizabeth[4] had twelve children:

a. Thomas Jefferson[4] Dovel

born on February 14, 1828 in Shenandoah County, Virginia. He died, age 78, on December 18, 1906 at Alma, Page County, Virginia. He married Amanda Virginia Kite on May 10, 1855 in Page County, Virginia. She was born on February 15, 1838 in Page County, Virginia. She died on January 23, 1899 in Page County, Virginia. Her father was John [Martin, William {of Orange County, Virginia}, John Windle {of Philadelphia, Pennsylvania}, James] Kite of Rockingham County, Virginia. Her mother was Delilah "Delia" [Johannes {Ermentradt of Rockingham County, Virginia}] Armentrout of Rockingham County, Virginia. Thomas[4] and Amanda had seven children: William A.[5], Charles H.[5] (or M.), Isaac Newton[5], (child)[5], Mittie[5], Ernest[5] and Clarence[5].

b. James M.[4] Dovel

born in 1829 in Shenandoah County, Virginia. He died, age 88, on October 19, 1917 in Page County, Virginia. He married Clara V.[4] Dovel [a cousin] circa 1860 in Rockingham County, Virginia. She was born circa 1836 in Rockingham County, Virginia. Her date and place of

178

death is not known. Her father was Tandy E.[3] [Daniel[2], David S.[1] {of England}] Dovel of Rockingham County, Virginia. Her mother was Catherine Lamb of Virginia. James[4] and Clara[4] had six children: James Robert[5], Laura E.[5], Lucious B.[5], Alice V.[5], Charles[5] and Sallie[5].

c. Cinderella[4] Dovel

born on December 23, 1832 in Page County, Virginia. She died, age 58, on April 5, 1891 in Page County, Virginia. She married John W. Snyder on September 18, 1848 in Page County, Virginia. He was born on February 21, 1826 in Page County, Virginia. He died, age 43, on January 23, 1870 at Stanley, Page County, Virginia and was buried there in the Graves Chapel Cemetery. His father was John Snyder of Madison County, Virginia. His mother was Judith Graves of Virginia. Cinderella[4] and John had seven children: Thomas Gilbert, Daniel Russell, William Trenton, Emma Blanche, Bettie Lee, David Benton and Lillie Byrd.

d. Charles Harrison[4] Dovel

born on May 4, 1834 in Page County, Virginia. He died, age 66, on February 3, 1900 in Page County, Virginia. He married, first, Minerva J. Stevens in 1855 in Page County, Virginia. She was born in 1835 in Virginia. Her date an place of death is not known. The name of her father and mother is not known. Charles^4 and Minerva had a child: Richard A.^{5}

Charles^4 married, second, Elizabeth Adeline^5 Ruffner on September 19, 1865 in Page County, Virginia. She was born on January 18, 1837 in Page County, Virginia. She died, age 58, on May 13, 1893 at Mt. Jackson, Shenandoah County, Virginia. Her father was Mark^4 [Jonas^3 {of Shenandoah County, Virginia}, Peter^2, Peter^1 {of Kingdom of Hanover, Germany}, Jakob^{1a} {of Maienfield, Germany}, Burhart^{2a}, George^{3a}, Hans^{4a}, Georg^{5a} {born circa 1545}] Ruffner of Page County, Virginia. Her mother was Lydia [Ulerick Abraham {of Lancaster County, Pennsylvania}, Christian] Biedler of Page County, Virginia. Charles^4 and Elizabeth^5 had eleven children: Henry Hunter^5, Robert M.^{5}, Charles P.^{5}, Henry Harper^5, Martha^5, Mary Alice^5, Viola V.^{5}, Marcelus^5, Nannie^5, Bettie Lee^5 and Annie K.^{5}

Elizabeth^5 had married, first, Samuel Holtzman on August 10, 1855 in Page County, Virginia. He was born in 1827 in Virginia. He died on November 29, 1859 in Cass County, Illinois. His father was William [Andrew] Holtzman of Maryland. His mother was Ruth Batman of Virginia. Elizabeth[5] and Samuel had two children: William Mark and Charles Thomas.

Charles[4] married, third, Betty Hultzman. There was no issue.

e. David T.[4] [afa David F.] Dovel

born on January 15, 1836 in Page County, Virginia. He died, age 77, on January 25, 1908 at Harrisonburg, Rockingham County, Virginia. He married Sarah Jane Summers on January 15, 1887 in Page County, Virginia. She was born on December 21, 1840 in Page County, Virginia. She died, age 75, on June 11, 1916, presumably in Rockingham County, Virginia. Her father was George W. [Michael] Summers of Page County, Virginia. Her mother was Susannah Hollingsworth of Shenandoah County, Virginia. David[4] and Sarah had eight children: William Eugene[5], George Ernest[5], Susie[5], Hattie[5], Bessie Blanche[5], Frank Lester[5], Lucie B.[5] and Fred L.[5].

f. Drucilla[4] Dovel

born on March 7, 1838 in Page County, Virginia.

She died, age 69, on April 21, 1907 in Page County, Virginia. She married Emmanuel Snyder on January 18, 1855 at the residence of Charles C.[3] Dovel in Page County, Virginia. He was born on September 17, 1821 at Page County, Virginia. He died on September 7, 1903 in Page County, Virginia. His father was John Snyder of Madison County, Virginia. His mother was Judith Graves of Virginia. Issue, if any, is not known.

g. Joseph Milton[4] Dovel

born on March 26, 1840 at Stanely, Page County, Virginia. He died, age 80, in 1920 in Shelby County, Ohio and was buried there in the Pasco Cemetery near Sidney. He married Mary Largent circa 1866 in Page County, Virginia. She was born on July 16, 1851 in Champagne County, Ohio. She died in April 1931 at Pemberton, Shelby County, Ohio. Her father was Henry Largent of Champagne County, Ohio. Her mother was Elizabeth (Unknown) of Champagne County, Ohio. Joseph[4], age 21, a farmer, enlisted in the CSA during the USCW at Luray, Virginia as a private on July 1, 1861 in Company D, 7th Cavalry, Regiment of Virginia. He reenlisted on April 4, 1962 and was promoted to full sergeant. Joseph[4] and Mary had six children:

182

Lydia E.[5], William D.[5], John Henry[5], Oliver C.[5], Della M.[5] and Felicia Mary[5].

h. Isaac C.[4] Dovel

born on July 2, 1842 in Page County, Virginia. He died, age 74, in 1916 in Champagne County, Ohio and was buried there on October 5, 1916 in the Myrtle Tree Cemetery at St. Paris. He married Louisa A.[7] Kite on July 25, 1868 in Champagne County, Ohio. She was born on September 12, 1851 in Champagne County, Ohio. She died on July 5, 1942 in Champagne County, Ohio and was buried there in the Myrtle Tree Cemetery at St. Paris. Her father was David[6] [Benjamine[5] {of Rockingham County, Virginia}, Adam[4], William[3], James[2] {of Blockley, Philadelphia County, Pennsylvania}, James[1] {of Chipping Campden, Gloucester, England}, Thomas[1a], Thomas[2a]] Kite of Champagne County, Ohio. Her mother was Sarah Jane [William Martin] Frank of Mad River Township, Champagne County, Ohio. Isaac[4] enlisted as a private in the CSA during the USCW on August 10, 1861 and remained until 1865 when he was wounded at Walden Railroad in Virginia during a charge. Isaac[4] and Louisa[7] had four children: Clara E.[5], Charles Russell[5], Lillian M.[5] and David Walter[5].

i.   Priscilla[4] Dovel

born on August 24, 1845 at Locust Dale, Madison County, Virginia. She died, age 69, on September 17, 1894 at Reno, Washoe County, Nevada. She married Jacob Franklin "Jake" Burner on August 3, 1863 at Locust Dale, Madison County, Virginia. He was born on July 10, 1840 in Page County, Virginia. He died on August 24, 1891 at Oroville, Butte County, California. His father was John Rhodes [Joseph, Jacob] Burner of Shenandoah County, Virginia. His mother was Susannah[3] "Susan" [Henry[2] {of Luray, Frederick County, Virginia}, Johann Henrich[1] "Henry" {of Muesen, Nassau-Siegen, Prussia}, Johannes[1a] {Brombach}, Christophel[2a], Caspar[3a], Jost[4a], Hans[5a] {In Der Brambach}, Jost[6a], Tilman[7a], Der Schn[8a] {born circa 1495}] Brumbach of Page County, Virginia. Priscilla[4] and Jacob had eleven children: Elizabeth, Carol, Viola Virginia, Frank Victor, Jacob, Jr, Junia C., Nevada May, John Charles, Grace Susan Darling, Hallie Bessie and Priscilla Janet.

j.   Russell T.[4] [afa Ruffner T.] Dovel

born on October 24, 1849 in Caroline County, Virginia. He died on October 21, 1933 in Champagne County, Ohio. He married Alitha Offenbacker sometime before September 1895 [when their first child was born], presumably in Champagne County, Ohio. She was born on January 22, 1852 in Champagne County, Ohio. She died on October 23, 1929 in Darke County, Ohio. Her father was Isaiah Offenbacker of Champagne County, Ohio. Her mother was Mahala Lung of Champagne County, Ohio. Russell[4] and Alitha had a child: Harry Russell[5].

k. Perry D.[4] Dovel

born in 1852 in Caroline County, Virginia. His date of death, sometime between 1920 and 1930 at Elko, Elko County, Nevada, is not known.

l. Jacob Randolph Tucker[4] Dovel

born on March 27, 1856 [another researcher says April 5, 1855] at Luray, Page County, Virginia. He died, age 64, on November 20, 1920 at Pickerington, Fairfield County, Ohio and was buried at Canal, Winchester County, Ohio. He married Olive Elizabeth "Lizzie Olive" Morton on September 9, 1896 at Pickerington, Fairfield County, Ohio. She was born on May 12, 1868 at Pickerington, Fairfield County, Ohio. She died on February 19, 1915 at Pickerington, Fairfield County, Ohio. Her father was Anthony Wayne Morton of Fairfield County, Ohio. Her mother was Elizabeth Dovel of Fairfield County, Ohio. Jacob[4] and Olive had a child: Elizabeth Marie[5].

Jacob[4] married, second, Alice Valentine on March 17, 1917 in Fairfield County, Ohio. She was born on June 11, 1876. Her place of birth is not known. She died on May 23, 1963 at Nashville, Davidson/Shelby County, Tennessee. The name of her father and mother is not known. Jacob[4] was a hotelier, a tobacco salesman and a farmer. He was a prominent man of Pickerington, Fairfield County, Ohio. Jacob[4] and Alice had a child: Grace Viola[5].

6. David Moncell[3] Dovel
born on September 21, 1819 at Alma, Rockingham County, Virginia. He died of heart disease on March 5, 1871 at Honey Run, Page County, Virginia. He married Elizabeth F. M. Booton on December 13, 1842 [another record says 1841] in Page County, Virginia. She was born on September 2, 1825 in Page County, Virginia. She died on February 27, 1901 in Page County, Virginia. Her father was "Elder" Ambrose C. [John K. {of Culpeper County and later of Madison County, Virginia}, Ambrose, William, Joshua {born 1670}] Booton of Orange County and later of Page County, Virginia. Her mother was Elizabeth [John

V. {of Shenandoah County, Virginia}] Fry of Jefferson County, Virginia. David[3] and Elizabeth had eleven children:

a. Mary Susan[4] Dovel

born on December 2, 1843 in Page County, Virginia. She died, age 87, on February 10, 1931 at Liberty, Holt County, Missouri. She married Hiram Godfrey[5] Nauman on November 16, 1871 in Page County, Virginia. He was born on March 20, 1847 in Page County, Virginia. He died, age 66, on January 17, 1914 at Liberty, Holt County, Missouri. His father was Reuben[4] [David O.[3] {of Shenandoah County, Virginia}, John Christian[2] {of Pennsylvania}, Johannes "John" Gottlieb[1] {of Hanover, Germany}, Johannes[1a]] Nauman of Page County, Virginia. His mother was Elizabeth[3] [Peter[2], David S.[1] {of England}] Dovel of Shenandoah County, Virginia. Mary[4] and Hiram[5] had six children: Stella Beuford[6], Carl Victor[6], Lelia Clide[6], Emma V.[6], Hiram Elmer[6] and Mary Bessie[6].

Hiram[5] had married, first, Eleanora Catherine[6] Kite on February 5, 1870 in Page County, Virginia. She was born on July 1, 1845 in Page County, Virginia. She died, age 24, on September 29, 1870 in Page County, Virginia and was buried there at Alma. Her father was Noah B.[5] [Benjamin[4], William[3] {of Orange County, Virginia}, John Windle[2], James[1] {of Chipping, Campden, Gloucestershire, England}, George[1a] {of Milton, Keynes, Buckinghamshire, England}, William[2a], Rychard[3a] {born circa 1580}] Kite of Page County, Virginia. Her mother was Isabella Virginia[4] [Henry[3], John[2], Henry[1] {of Switzerland}] Pirkey of Grove Hill, Rockingham County, Virginia. There was no issue.

b. William Tazewell[4] Dovel

born on June 14, 1846 in Page County, Virginia. He died, age 70, on August 16, 1916 at Craig, Holt County, Missouri. He married Eliza E.[5] Nauman on January 30, 1983 in Page County, Virginia. She was born circa 1848 in Page County, Virginia. She died, age 85, in December 1933 in Holt County, Missouri. Her father was Reuben[4] [David O.[3] {of Shenandoah County, Virginia}, John Christian[2] {of Pennsylvania}, Johannes "John" Gottlieb[1] {of Hanover, Germany}, Johannes[1a]] Nauman of Page County, Virginia. Her mother was Elizabeth[3] [Peter[2], David S.[1], {of England}] Dovel of Shenandoah County, Virginia. William[4] and Eliza[5] had four children: William H.[5], Mary B.[5], Annie K.[5] and Harry Perrin[5].

c. Rebecca E.[4] Dovel

born circa 1848 in Page County, Virginia. Her date and place of death is not known. She married John D.[1] Andes on June 20, 1867 in Page County, Virginia. He was born in 1840 in London, England. His date and place of death is not known. His father was James[1a] Andes of England. His mother was Mary Ann[1a] (Unknown) of England. Issue, if any, is not known.

d. Viola E.[4] Dovel

born circa 1850 at the Shenandoah Iron Works, Page County, Virginia. Her date and place of death is not known. She married Andrew J. Welfley on December 3, 1863 in Page County, Virginia. He was born in 1848 in Page County, Virginia. His date and place of death is not known. His father was John Welfley of Page County, Virginia. His mother was Mary Catherine [Jacob] Roudabush of Shenandoah, Page County, Virginia. Viola[4] and Andrew had two children: John D. M. and Virgil Eugene.

e. Lewis Cass Clark[4] Dovel

born on June 24, 1852 in Page County, Virginia. He died, age 84, in August 1936 at Maitland,

Holt County, Missouri. He married, first, Sarah Catherine Keyser[5] Housden on March 24, 1880 in Page County, Virginia. She was born in 1863 in Page County, Virginia. She died in 1897 at Dovel Hollow, Page County, Virginia and was buried there in the Keyser Cemetery. Her father was (Unknown) Keyser of Page County, Virginia. Her mother was Formasanta[4] [Benjamin Dovel[3], Judith[2] {Dovel of Culpeper County, Virginia}, Benjamin[1] {of Lambeth, England}, William[1a]] Housden of Page County, Virginia. Lewis[4] and Sarah[5] had eleven children: James Clark[5], Mary Elizabeth[5], John Weston[5] [afa Wesley], Martha Frances[5], Minerva C.[5], Maude May[5], Joseph Edward[5], David Moncell[5], Taswell Orville[5], Martin[5] and William[5].

Lewis[4] married, second, Elizabeth Leon circa 1897/1898, presumably in Page County, Virginia [Editor's Note: Lewis[4] and Sarah Catherine Keyser[5] Housden's son, David Moncell[5] Dovel married an Ora Leon; the ancestral connection is not known]. Her date and place of birth and death is not known. The name of her father and mother is not known. Issue, if any, is not known.

f. Emma F.[4] Dovel

born circa 1854 in Page County, Virginia. Her date and place of death is not known. She married Abraham[5] Strickler on December 24, 1874 in Page County, Virginia. He was born on October 24, 1853 in Page County, Virginia. He died, age 62, on March 23, 1910, probably in Iowa. His father was David[4] [Martin[3], John[2], Abraham[1] {of Zurich, Switzerland}] Strickler of Virginia. His mother was Mary[3] "Polly" [Philip[2], Heinrich[1] {of Germany}] Kibler of Shenandoah County, Virginia. Emma[4] and Abraham[5] had a child: Walter D.[6]

Abraham[5] married, second, Effie Amner Flock on February 1, 1888 in Iowa. She was born on January 9, 1866 in Iowa. She died in 1939, presumably in Kansas. Her father was John Fankbower [Mathias {of New Jersey}, John {Flack}, Mathias {Flach}, Andreas {of Flocktown, German Valley and later of Long Valley, Rosbury Township, New Washington County, New Jersey}] Flock of Tuscarawas County, Ohio. Her mother was Caroline Amner [Joseph {of Virginia and later of Fulton County, Arkansas}] Ramsey of St. Louis, St. Louis City County, Missouri. Abraham[5] and Effie had four children: Earl Jasper[6], Opal Blanche[6], Ruby May[6] and Emerald Felicia[6].

g. Virgil C.[4] Dovel

born circa 1856 at the Shenandoah Iron Works, Page County, Virginia. His date and place of death is not known. He married Lusette "Lisetta" (Unknown) circa 1899, probably in Custer County, Oklahoma. She was born circa 1872 in Nebraska. Her date and place of death is not known. On September 28, 1903, Virgil[4] received a U. S. Land Patent recorded in Book A-P, Page 121, thought to be part of the Oklahoma land rush lands. Virgil[4] and Lusette had two children; Edith Leota[5] and Marvella G.[5] [although some researchers believe Edith Leota[5] was a child of Lusette's from a previous marriage].

h. (child)[4] Dovel

born circa 1857 at the Shenandoah Iron Works, Page County, Virginia. The child's date and place of death is not known.

i. Laura E.[4] Dovel

born on April 9, 1859 at the Shenandoah Iron Works, Page County, Virginia. She died, age 71, on March 6, 1931 at the Shenandoah Iron Works, Page County, Virginia and was buried there in the Graves Chapel Cemetery at Stanley.

She married Samuel Ernest[7] Kite on November 18, 1880 in Page County, Virginia. He was born on December 11, 1858 in Page County, Virginia. He died, age 69, on November 28, 1928 in Page County, Virginia and was buried there in the Graves Chapel Cemetery at Stanley. His father was Jacob R.[6] [Jacob C.[5], Martin[4] {of Heidelberg, Berks County, Pennsylvania}, William[3] {of Rockingham County, Virginia}, James[2] {of Philadelphia, Philadelphia County, Pennsylvania}, James[1] {of Chipping Campden, Gloucestershire, England}, George[1a] {of Newport Pagnell, Buckinghamshire, England}] Kite of Page County, Virginia. His mother was Sarah Jane Lionberger of Page County, Virginia. Laura[4] and Samuel[7] had six children: Clarette[8], Harry A.[8], Frederick E.[8], Samuel[8], Myrtle Hellene[8] and Lloyd A.[8].

j. Joseph E. J.[4] Dovel

born circa 1861/1862 at the Shenandoah Iron Works, Page County, Virginia. He died, age 51, on February 22, 1912 at St. Louis, St. Louis County, Missouri. His death certificate indicated he was a conductor [presumably on a train]. He probably never married.

k. Lulu S.[4] Dovel

born circa 1866 at the Shenandoah Iron Works, Page County, Virginia. Her date and place of death is not known.

[EDITOR'S NOTE: The Shenandoah Iron Works, which later became the town of Shenandoah, were furnaces built by the Forrer brothers. In effect, it was a company town where workers lived, worked and many times paid for purchases at the company store by working it off {sort of like the payday loans of today}.]

The Life and Times of
David S.[1] Dovel, Sr.

PATERNAL ANCESTRY: [DOVEL: (Unknown)]

MATERNAL ANCESTRY: [(UNKNOWN)]

[EDITOR'S NOTE: This family, whose name was originally found as Deauville and Duvall, purportedly migrated from France to England after King Louis IV revoked the Edict of Nantes, which was issued in 1598 by King Henry IV to provide freedom of religious worship for Protestants; One researcher claims the family originated in French Guiana].

DAVID S.[1], Sr. was born circa 1728 in England. He died circa 1807 at Ingham, Rockingham County, Virginia. The name of his father is not known. The name of his mother is not known [Editor's Note: Some researchers list his father and mother as Charles and Millicent Dovel of Maryland; however, the dates listed are at odds with David[1]'s date of birth].

DAVID S.[1], Sr., age 20, married Barbara Blosser, age 15, of Caroline, Rockingham County, Virginia in 1748, presumably at Caroline, Rockingham County, Virginia. She was born circa 1733 at Caroline, Rockingham County, Virginia. She died circa 1820 in Rockingham County, Virginia and was buried at the Dovel homesite in Rockingham [now Page] County, Virginia. The name of her father and mother is not known.

[EDITOR'S NOTE: The area the Dovel families settled in Rockingham County, Virginia later became part of Page County; Page county was formed in 1831 from sections of Rockingham and Shenandoah Counties]

DAVID S.[1], Sr., a farmer by trade, arrived in America from England with his brother William[1] in 1745. The original homestead was at a place that became known as Dovel Mountain. Dovel Mountain is a mountain summit in Page County in the state of Virginia. The mountain climbs to 2,448 feet [746.15 meters] above sea level. Dovel Mountain is located in the Shenandoah National Forest at Shenandoah, Virginia at GPS co-ordinates of N 38.517624 and W 78.552512.

[EDITOR'S NOTE: From Washington, D.C. take 66 west to Route 81 South, Exit 264 to Route 211 East (to New Market) to South on Route 340 to Left on Route 650 (Grove Hill River Road) to Right onto Ingham Lane to Shenandoah, Virginia]

The Children of
David S.[1] Dovel, Sr.
and Barbara Blosser

1. George[2] Dovel
born circa 1752 at Alma, Rockingham County,
Virginia. His date and place of death is not known.
He married Ann Peeksly [sometimes found as
Peeksby] on April 11, 1807 in Page County, Virginia [he age 57, she age 39]. She was born circa
1770 at Stanley, Page County, Virginia. She died in
1802, presumably in Page County, Virginia. Her
father was Christian Peeksly of Rockingham
County, Virginia. The name of her mother is not
known. George[2] and Ann had three children:

a. Margaret[3] "Peggy" Dovel
born on October 18, 1809 in Page County,
Virginia. She died, age 73, in November 1882 in
Page County, Virginia. She married Asa Alger
on February 18, 1833 in Page County, Virginia.
He was born on September 18, 1808 in Page
County, Virginia. He died on September 13,
1867 in Page County, Virginia. His father was
Abraham Lemuel Alger of Page County,
Virginia. His mother was Anna Magdalena
[Valentine {Schneider of Pennsylvania}] Snyder
[afa Snider] of Page County, Virginia. Margaret[3]
and Asa had nine children: Andrew W.J., Mary

197

Ann, Isaac, Barbara A., Nathaniel, Elizabeth Jane, Martha, James Harvey and Abraham.

b. Nancy[3] Dovel

born on February 8, 1811 in Page County, Virginia. She died, age 102, in 1913 at Shenandoah, Page County, Virginia. She married John[4] Dofflemyer on April 19, 1832 at Luray, Page County, Virginia. He was born on April 10, 1810 in Page County, Virginia. He died, age 74, on April 10, 1884 at Cub Run, Page County, Virginia. His father was Henry D.[3] [Michael[2] {Tofflemier of Mannackies, Frederick County, Maine}, Johannes[1] {Taffelmeyer of Bishcollsheim, Sinsheim, Baden, Germany}, Andreas[1a] {Deffelmeyer of Oberlen-ningen, Donaukreis, Wurtemberg, Germany}, David[2a] {Tafelmeyer}]] Dofflemyer of Page County, Virginia. His mother was Elizabeth Snyder of Page County, Virginia. Nancy[3] and John[4] had nine children: William A.[5], Daniel H.[5], Mary Jane[5], James H.[5], Elizabeth A.[5], B.F.[5], Nancy A.[5], John Wesley[5] and George W.[5].

c. Adam Beauregard[3] Dovel

born on April 30, 1814 at Shenandoah, Page County, Virginia. He died, age 65, at Stanley, Page County, Virginia. He married Diana Shuler on September 30, 1835 in Page County,

Virginia. She was born on October 17, 1819 in Page County, Virginia. She died, age 102, on April 28, 1922 at Ingham, Page County, Virginia. Her father was George [John, John Matthias {of Pennsylvania}] Shuler of Shenandoah County, Virginia. Her mother was Talitha[3] [David S.[2], Jr., David S.[1] {of England}] Dovel of Caroline County, Virginia. Adam[3] and Diana had ten children: Talitha Jane[4], George Decatur[4], Isaac Newton[4], Susan E.[4], Susan Kern[4], Alonzo L.[4], Diana Rebecca[4], Julia[4], Lovenia[4] and Adam B.[4].

[Editor's Note: Some researchers list a fourth child, Peggy[3], born 1818, but seems odd since Margaret[3] "Peggy" was still alive at that time and is probably one in the same].

2. Bolser[2] Dovel
   born on March 20, 1755 at Alma, Rockingham County, Virginia. His date of death in Orange County, Virginia is not known. He married Nancy[2] Greening on March 12, 1798 in Albemarle County, Virginia. She was born circa 1755 in Albemarle County, Virginia. Her date of death in Orange County, Virginia is not known. Her father was Robert Frank[1] Greening of Ireland and later of Albemarle County, Virginia. Her mother was Sarah[3] [John[2] {of Greenfield, Orange County,

Virginia}, Thomas[1] {of England}]] Dowell of Albemarle County, Virginia. Issue, if any, is not known.

3. **David S.[2] Dovel, Jr.**
born on April 15, 1768 at Alma, Rockingham, Virginia. He died in February 1832 at Alma, Page County, Virginia. He married Keziah Short circa 1793 in Rockingham County, Virginia. She was born on August 20, 1774 in Virginia. She died sometime between 1850 and 1860 in Page County, Virginia. Her father was Samuel [Samuel, Samuel {of Rappahannock County, Virginia}, Thomas] Short of Virginia. Her mother was Hannah (Unknown). David[2] and Keziah had six children: William[3], Talitha[3], John W.[3], Daniel D.[3], Charles C.[3] and David Moncell[3].

4. Daniel[2] Dovel
born on March 20, 1773 at Alma, Rockingham County, Virginia. He died on May 18, 1827 in Rockingham County, Virginia and was buried there in the Frieden's Church Cemetery. He married Catherine[3] Miller sometime before 1801 [when their first child was born] in Rockingham County, Virginia. She was born on February 16, 1766 in Page County, Virginia. She died on October 13, 1830 at Mt. Crawford, Rockingham County, Virginia. Her father was Christian[2] [Adam[1] {of Schriesheim, Rhein-Necker-Kreis,

Baden-Wuerttemberg, Germany}, Johann Peter[1a] {Mueller of Pfalzdorf, Kleve, Nordhein, Westfalen, Germany}, Johann Jacob[2a], Jost Friedrich[3a], Johannes[4a], Johannes[5a], Johannes[6a], Thoenies[7a] {born circa 1600}] Miller of Rockingham County, Virginia. Her mother was Anna Catherine[2] [Johann Stephen[1] {of Germany}, Johannes[1a] {of Heringen, Nassau, Hessen, Germany}, Hans Jacob[2a], Hans Dietrich[3a]] Conrad of Berkshire County, Pennsylvania. Daniel[2] and Catherine[3] had two children:

a. Tandy E.[3] Dovel
    born on March 9, 1801 at Mt. Crawford, Rockingham County, Virginia. He died, age 70, on April 9, 1891 at Mt. Crawford, Rockingham County, Virginia. He married Catherine Lamb in 1827 at Mt. Crawford, Rockingham County, Virginia. She was born in 1810 in Virginia. She died, age 88, in 1898 at Mt. Crawford, Rockingham County, Virginia. The name of her father and mother is not known. Tandy[3] and Catherine had fourteen children: Malinda[4], Catherine Urilla[4], Clara V.[4], Absolom[4], Jeremiah[4], Clara V.[4], Lucious Bonaparte[4], Susan R.[4], Tandy E.[4], Thomas J.[4], David Alpheus[4], John Howard[4], James N.[4] and Laura M.[4].

    It seems that Tandy[3] and his family were Union Loyalists during the Civil War. They were supposedly threatened many times by the rebels and two of the boys were arrested and several times were taken away for the army. Each time they ran away. In October 1864, General Sheridan of the Union Army encamped nearby for about three weeks and took 40 hogs, 4 horses, many cattle, tobacco, corn and wood, for which the family was eventually paid for over ten years later.

b. James[3] Dovel
born on February 2, 1803 at Mt. Crawford, Rockingham County, Virginia. He died, age 46, on May 18, 1849 at Mt. Crawford, Rockingham County, Virginia. He married Barbara Yount circa 1823 in Rockingham County, Virginia. She was born circa 1803 in Virginia. She died on July 28, 1863 at Melrose, Rockingham County, Virginia. The name of her father and mother is not known. James[3] and Barbara had a child: Mary Elizabeth[4].

5. John Sylvannus[2] Dovel
born on September 15, 1776 at Alma, Rockingham County, Virginia. He died, age 82, on February 23, 1859 at Pickering, Fairfield County, Ohio and was buried at Violet Township, Franklin County, Ohio. He married Grace Marie[6] Looker on May 29, 1817 at Rockingham County, Virginia. She was born on

March 21, 1783 in Augusta County, Virginia. She died on December 21, 1834 at Pickering, Fairfield County, Ohio and was buried at Violet Township, Franklin County, Ohio. Her father was John[5] [Thomas[4] {of Elizabethtown, Union County, New Jersey}, William[3], William[2] {of New York}, Henry[1] {of Bures St. Mary, Suffolk, England, then later of Sudbury, Middlesex County, Massachusetts}, Henry[1a], Robert[2a], John[3a], Robert[4a]] Looker of Rockingham County, Virginia. Her mother was Frances [Michael {of Culpeper County, Virginia}] Russell of Augusta County, Virginia. John[2] and Grace[6] had at least four children and possible a fifth child [not counting Abraham Morton[3]]:

a. Abraham Morton[3] Dovel
born in 1807 in Virginia. [Editor's Note: Most researchers believe that Grace[6] Looker may have been married earlier to, or had a child with, an (Unknown) Morton, and that Abraham[3] is their offspring who later assumed the name Dovel]. He died [per a death record] on October 25, 1853 at Story Run, Page County, Virginia [another researcher claims he died on March 4, 1888]. He married Harriet Short on June 22, 1833 in Page County, Virginia. She was born in 1807 in Virginia. She died in 1838 in Virginia. Her father was William Short of Page County, Virginia. The name of her mother is not

known. Abraham[3] and Harriet had a child: Alexander Hambiltonian[4].

b. Anna[3] Dovel
born in 1818 in Rockingham County, Virginia. She died, age 42, in November 1860 in Fairfield County, Ohio. She married James R. Looker circa 1837 in Fairfield County, Ohio. He was born on January 27, 1822 in Fairfield County, Ohio. He died, age 78, on September 15, 1900 in Fairfield County, Ohio. His father was Joseph Looker of Rockingham County, Virginia. His mother was Charlotte Okane of Rockingham County, Virginia. Anna[3] and James had six children: Grace Ann, John, Mary, Andrew, Scott and James R.

c. Lucina[3] Dovel
born on March 18, 1819 in Rockingham County, Virginia. She died, age 55, on September 18, 1874 at Pickerington, Fairfield County, Ohio. She married Andrew Jackson[3] Dovel [her cousin] on March 11, 1854 in Fairfield County, Ohio. He was born on September 14, 1818 in Page County, Virginia. He died, age 69, on March 8, 1888 in Fairfield County, Ohio. His father was Peter[2] [David S.[1] {of England}] Dovel of Ingham, Rockingham County, Virginia. His mother was Elizabeth [John {of Lancaster

County, Virginia}] Keyser of Shenandoah County, Virginia. Issue, if any, is not known.

d. Frances[3] Dovel
born on October 9, 1820 in Rockingham County, Virginia. She died, age 78, on March 8, 1899 at Pickering, Fairfield County, Ohio. She married Andrew French on October 14, 1836 in Fairfield County, Ohio. He was born in 1818 at Pickering, Fairfield County, Ohio. He died, age 76, on August 13, 1894 at Pickering, Fairfield County, Ohio. His father was David [Patrick] French of Fairfield County, Ohio. His mother was Martha [Joseph] Anderson of Fairfield County, Ohio. Frances[3] and Andrew had eight children: Benjamin Franklin, Elizabeth, George, Grace, Jenny, John, Lucinda and Martha.

e. Elizabeth D.[3] Dovel
born on November 29, 1821 in Rockingham County, Virginia. She died, age 74, on October 26, 1896 in Fairfield County, Ohio. She married Jacob Benjamin[3] "Jake" Dovel [her cousin] on January 11, 1837 at Luray, Page County, Virginia. He was born on September 16, 1816, probably at Luray, Page County, Virginia. He died, age 65, on December 2, 1901 in Fairfield County, Ohio. His father was Peter[2] [David S.[1] {of England}] Dovel of Ingham, Rockingham

County, Virginia. His mother was Elizabeth [John {of Lancaster County, Virginia}] Keyser of Shenandoah County, Virginia. Elizabeth[3] and Benjamin[3] had nine children: Olive Virginia[4], Adelaide[4], Lydia[4], John[4], Elizabeth[4], Lucinda Theodosia[4] "Lucy," Andrew Jackson[4], Florence Ann[4] "Florida" and Benjamin Franklin[4] "Frank."

[Editor's Note: There was possibly a sixth child: Rosie M.[3] Dovel; however, no further record has been found]

6. Peter[2] [afa Peter A.] Dovel
born on April 2, 1777 at Alma, Rockingham County, Virginia. He died on April 19, 1870 at Stanley, Page County, Virginia and was buried in St. Peter's Church Cemetery in Page County, Virginia. He married, first, Elizabeth Ann Kiser [afa Keyser and Kysor] on August 28, 1807 in Rockingham County, Virginia. She was born circa 1782 in Rockingham County, Virginia. She died in 1831 in Page County, Virginia and was buried there in the Keyser Cemetery in Dovel Hollow. Her father was John Keyser [afa Kaiser] of Lancaster County, Pennsylvania and later of Rockingham County, Virginia. The name of her mother is not known. Peter[2] and Elizabeth had nine children:

a. Isaac C.[3] Dovel
    born on December 12, 1811 in Page County,
    Virginia. He died, age 68, on December 21, 1879
    at Iron Town, Lawrence County, Ohio.

b. Abraham[3] Dovel
    born on August 11, 1813 at Shenandoah
    County, Virginia. He died, age 74, on April 3,
    1888 in Page County, Virginia. He married
    Harriet Short on June 30, 1833 in Page County,
    Virginia. She was born circa 1812 in Virginia.
    Her date and place of death is not known. The
    name of her father and mother is not known.
    Abraham[3] and Harriet had five children:
    Charlotte Jane[4], Alexander N.[4], Fereta F.[4], Sarah
    C.[4] and Rebecca Susan[4].

c. Jacob Benjamin[3] "Jake" Dovel
    born September 19, 1816 at Honeyville, Page
    County, Virginia. He died, age 85, in Fairfield
    County, Ohio. He married Elizabth[3] Dovel [his
    cousin] on January 11, 1837 at Luray, Page
    County, Virginia. She was born on November
    29, 1821 in Rockingham County, Virginia. She
    died, age 74, on October 26, 1896 in Fairfield
    County, Ohio. Her father was John Sylvanus[2]
    [David S.[1] {of England}] Dovel of Page County,
    Virginia. Her mother was Grace Marie[6] [John[5],
    Thomas[4] {of Elizabethtown, Union County,

New Jersey}, William[3], William[2] {of New York}, Henry[1] {of Bures St. Mary, Suffolk, England, then later of Sudbury, Middlesex County, Massachusetts}, Henry[1a], Robert[2a], John[3a], Robert[4a]] Looker of Rockingham County, Virginia. Jacob[3] and Elizabeth[3] had nine children: Olive Virginia[4], Adelaide[4], Lydia[4], John[4], Elizabeth[4], Lucinda Theodosia[4] "Lucy," Andrew Jackson[4], Florence Ann[4] "Florida" and Benjamin Franklin[4] "Frank."

d. Andrew Jackson[3] Dovel

born on September 14, 1818 in Page County, Virginia. He died, age 69, on March 8, 1888 in Fairfield County, Ohio. He married Lucina[3] Dovel [his cousin] on March 11, 1854 in Fairfield County, Ohio. She was born on March 18, 1819 in Rockingham County, Virginia. She died, age 55, on September 18, 1874 at Pickerington, Fairfield County, Ohio. Her father was John Sylvanus[2] [David S.[1] {of England}] Dovel of Page County, Virginia. Her mother was Grace Marie[6] [John[5], Thomas[4] {of Elizabethtown, Union County, New Jersey}, William[3], William[2] {of New York}, Henry[1] {of Bures St. Mary, Suffolk, England, then later of Sudbury, Middlesex County, Massachusetts}, Henry[1a], Robert[2a], John[3a], Robert[4a]] Looker of Rockingham County, Virginia. Issue, if any, is not known.

e. Anne Elizabeth[3] Dovel
born on November 5, 1820 in Page County, Virginia. She died, age 52, in Jasper County, Illinois. She married Ezra Adenston Mahaney on November 25, 1841 in Page County, Virginia. He was born on December 29, 1815 in Page County, Virginia. He died, age 63, on March 18, 18979 in Jasper County, Illinois. His father was Jeremiah Mahoney of Coleraine Township, Lancaster County, Pennsylvania and later of Bayview, Cecil County, Maryland. His mother was Elizabeth[3] [Johann Jacob[2] {of Rock Hill, Montgomery County, Pennsylvania}, Johann Jacob[1] {of Badin-Wuertemberg, Germany}]] Dadisman of Dover, York County, Pennsylvania. Anne[3] and Ezra had eight children: Peter Sullivan, Mary Elizabeth, Andrew J., John H., Joel Jeremiah, Jacob Zachariah, George Hiram and Dolly Jane.

f. Peter Simon[3] Dovel
born on August 8, 1921 in Page County, Virginia. He died, age 76, on February 9, 1903 at Stanley, Page County, Virginia and was buried there in the Seventh Day Adventist Cemetery. He married Elizabeth Margaret Petefish on October 27, 1859 in Page County, Virginia. She

was born on February 8, 1840 in Rockingham County, Virginia. She died on July 21, 1903 at Stanley, Page County, Virginia and was buried there in the Seventh Day Adventist Cemetery. Her father was Adam Petefish of Rockingham County, Virginia. Her mother was Amanda Jane (Unknown) of Virginia. Peter[3] enlisted and served in the CSA during the USCW between 1861 and 1865 in Company I, 97th Virginia Militia. Peter[3] and Elizabeth had five children: Viola J.[4], Charles Lee[4], Ella Barbara[4], Amanda Auvora[4] and Jacob Isaac[4].

[Editor's Note: Some researchers erroneously assign his father's third wife, Julia Ann Jenkins as Peter[3]'s second wife.]

g. Elizabeth[3] Dovel
born on November 21, 1824 in Page County, Virginia. She died, age 37, on April 3, 1861 in Caroline County, Virginia. She married Reuben[4] Nauman on December 28, 1843 in Page County, Virginia. He was born on November 10, 1887 in Holt County, Missouri. His father was David O.[3] [John Christian[2] {of Pennsylvania}, Johannes "John" Gottlieb[1] {of Hanover, Germany}, Johannes[1a]] Nauman of Shenandoah County, Virginia. His mother was Catherine [John] Sigler of Rockingham County, Virginia.

Elizabeth[3] and Reuben[4] had ten children: (child)[5], Joseph Sirus[5], Hiram Gilbert[5], Eliza E.[5] [who married William Tazewell[4] Dovel], Jacob Erasmus[5], Mary Catherine[5], Anna Barbara[5], Peter Simon[5], John William[5] and David Clinton[5].

h. Mary C.[3] Dovel
    born on September 27, 1826 in Page County, Virginia. Her date and place of death is not known.

i. Barbara A.[3] Dovel
    born on October 9, 1829 at Stanley, Page County, Virginia. She died, age 69, on May 20, 1898 in Caroline County, Virginia. She married Andrew Jackson Long on October 10, 1858 in Page County, Virginia. He was born on August 22, 1824, probably in Page County, Virginia. He died, age 67, on October 17, 1891 in Page County, Virginia. His father was Benjamin Long of Page County, Virginia. His mother was Mary Koontz of Page County, Virginia. Barbara[3] and Andrew had a child: Hampton Caspar.

j. John[3] Dovel
    born on December 25, 1830 in Page County, Virginia. He died, age 29, on February 3, 1859 at Pickering, Fairfield County, Ohio [another

researcher says he died on April 21, 1900 in Jasper County, Illinois]. He married Grace French in 1853 at Pickering, Fairfield County, Ohio. Her date and place of birth and death is not known. Her father was Andrew [David, Patrick] French of Pickering, Fairfield County, Ohio. Her mother was Frances[3] [John[2] {of Alma, Page County, Virginia}, David S.[1] {of England}] Dovel of Rockingham County, Virginia [Editor's Note: Frances[3] is John[3]'s first cousin]. John[3] and Grace had two children: John Clark[4] and Frances Ida[4].

Peter[2] married, second, Mary[3] "Marie" Norman {Housden} [Editor's Note: Apparently, the Housden surname was from an earlier marriage] on January 24, 1832, either in Shenandoah or Rockingham County, Virginia [Also, some researchers report a previous marriage to a James Dovel]. She was born circa 1780 in Shenandoah County, Virginia. She died circa 1850 in Shenandoah County, Virginia. Her father was John Christian[2] [Johannes "John" Gottlieb[1] {of Hanover, Germany}, Johannes[1a]] Norman [afa Nauman] of Lancaster County, Pennsylvania. Her mother was Christina[2] Frederich Johann[1] {of Tyrol, Austria}] Stoneberger of Shanandoah County, Virginia. Peter[2] and Mary[3] had no issue.

Peter² married, third, Julia Ann Jenkins on November 14, 1850 at Page County, Virginia. She was born in 1804 in Virginia. The date and place of her death is not known. The name of her father is not known. Her mother was Eula (Unknown). There was no issue.

7. Elizabeth² Dovel
born circa 1780 at Alma, Rockingham County, Virginia. She died sometime between 1840 and 1850 [another record suggests 1845] in Jackson County, Tennessee. She married Johannes³ "John" Propst [afa Propes] on May 20, 1800 in Rockingham County, Virginia. He was born circa 1770/ 1775 in Pendleton County, Virginia [now West Virginia]. He died sometime after 1850 [when he last appears on the U. S. Census] in Jackson County, Tennessee. His father was Frederick George² [Johann Michael¹ {of Germany}, Hans Michael¹ᵃ, Hans Michael²ᵃ, Johann³ᵃ] Propst of Rockingham County, Virginia. His mother was Barbara² [Marcus¹ "Mark" {of Baden-Wuerttemberg, Germany}] Swadley of Augusta, Hampshire County, Virginia [which later became part of West Virginia]. Elizabeth² and Johannes³ had six children:

b. Nancy⁴ Propst
born in February 1801 in Rockingham County,

Virginia. She died in 1850. Her place of death is not known.

c. John Dovel[4] Propst
born on August 19, 1804 [or 1805] in Pendleton County, Virginia. He died on April 30, 1874 at Romine Township, Marion County, Illinois. He married, first, Nancy Hefflin[2] Hagen circa 1822/1824 in Kentucky. She was born on February 20, 1801 in Virginia. She died on March 8, 1859 in Allen County, Kentucky. Her father was Arthur[1] "Red Art" Hagen of Ireland. Her mother was Lydia (Unknown) of Kentucky. John[4] and Nancy[2] had six children: John D.[5], Martha Ann[5], Elizabeth Dovel[5], Barney Hagen[5], Sylvanus[5] and Richard[5].

John[4] married, second, Margaret Grooms Penticuff on March 7, 1859 in Casey County, Kentucky. She was born circa 1810 in Virginia. Her date of death in Marion County, Illinois is not known. The name of her father and mother is not known. Issue, if any, is not known.

d. Samuel[4] Propst
born in 1805 in Jackson County, Tennessee. His date and place of death is not known [he may have died young].

e. James[4] Propst
   born in 1810 in Jackson County, Tennessee. His date and place of death is not known.

f. Lewis[4] Propst
   born in 1813 in Jackson County, Tennessee [another researcher says September 29, 1809] in Pendleton County, West Virginia. He died, age 61, on April 30, 1874 in Marion County, Illinois.

g. Sarah[4] Propst
   born in August 1815 in Jackson County, Tennessee. She died, age 85, on July 29, 1900 in Macon County, Tennessee. She may have had a child: R. Propst [born circa 1846 in Tennessee].

h. George B.[4] Propst
   born in 1823 in Jackson County, Tennessee. He died, age 35, in 1858 [another researcher says 1854] in Tennessee.

Johannes[1] had married, first, Margaret Naile in 1795, presumably in Rockingham County, Virginia. Apparently, they were divorced. She was born in 1776 in Virginia. She died, age 60, on July 14, 1836. Her place of death is not known. Johannes[1] and Margaret had a child:

a. Daniel[4] Propst
   born in 1796 in Virginia. He died, age 74, in 1870 in Kentucky.

8. Barbara[2] Dovel
   born circa 1792 at Alma, Rockingham County, Virginia. She died in 1829 at Caledonia, Washington County, Missouri. She, age 17, married Abraham[3] Ebersole, he age 23, on May 17, 1809 in Rockingham County, Virginia. He was born circa 1786 in Rockingham County, Virginia. He died in August 1829 at Caledonia, Washington County, Missouri. His father was Michael[2] [Abraham[1] {of Bern, Canton of Bern, Switzerland and later of Dauphin County, Pennsylvania}, Petere[1a] {Ebersohl of Friedelsheim, Bad Durkheim, Rheinland-Pfalz, Germany}, Jost[2a] {Ebersold of Musingen, Canton of Bern, Switzerland}, Jost[3a], Ulrich[4a] {Aebersold}, Ulrich[5a], Eulrigh[6a], Konrad[7a] {born 1513}] Eversole of Lancaster County, Pennsylvania, later of Rockingham County, Virginia, and finally of Hagerstown, Washington County, Maryland. His mother was Elizabeth (Unknown). Barbara[2] and Abraham[3] had six children:

a. (daughter)[4] Ebersole/Eversole
   born circa 1810 at Washington, Augusta County, Virginia. She apparently died young at Washington, Augusta County, Virginia.

b. George Harrison[4] Ebersole/Eversole born circa 1815 at Washington, Augusta County, Virginia. He died, age 57, on March 8, 1872 at St. Louis [city of], Missouri. He married Jane (Unknown). George[4] and Jane had a child: Georgiana[5] "Ann."

c. William Goforth[4] Ebersole/Eversole born on January 19, 1819 at Caledonia, Washington County, Missouri. He died on January 25, 1894 at Caledonia, Washington County, Missouri. He married Rebecca Anne[5] Rutledge on September 5, 1854 at Potosi, Washington County, Missouri. She was born on May 6, 1830 at Blacksburg, Montgomery County, Virginia. She died on November 4, 1909 at Farmington, St. Francois County, Missouri. Her father was James[4] [Edward[3] {of Augusta County, Virginia}, Thomas[2], George[1] {of Scotland, who later removed to Ireland}] Rutledge of Montgomery County, Virginia. Her mother was Nancy Ann[3] [Archibald[2] {of Bath County, Virginia}, William[1] {of County Down, Ireland}, William[1a] {of Scotland}, Archibald[2a], John[3a], Rees[4a], John[5a], Archibald[6a], William[7a], John[8a] {born circa 1458 in Scotland}, John[9a] {born circa 1425 in Denmark}] Thompson of Thompson Valley, Tazewell County, Virginia. William[4] and Rebecca[5] had eight children: Frank[5], Ettie E.[5], William E.[5],

George Harrison[5], William Goforth[5], Edward Thompson[5], Annie[5] and Jane L.[5] "Jennie."

d. Greenberry[4] "Berry" Ebersole/Eversole
born circa 1821 at Caledonia, Washington County, Missouri. He died in 1855 at Springfield, Greene County, Missouri. He married Polina (Unknown), she age 16, in 1849 in Missouri. She was born circa 1833 in Missouri. Her date and place of death is not known. Greenberry[4] and Polina had three children: Jenny[5], Greenberry A.[5] "Berry" and Susan[5].

e. Hardin N.[4] Ebersole/Eversole
born on June 12, 1825 at Caledonia, Washington County, Missouri. He died on February 17, 1918 at Lewiston, Lewis County, Missouri. He married Maria J. "Marie" Wainright Fleak sometime before 1855 [when their first child was born], presumably in Washington County, Missouri. She was born on February 14, 1824 in Kentucky. She died in 1905 at Lewiston, Lewis County, Missouri. The name of her father and mother is not known. Hardin[4] and Marie had five children: George[5], Josephine[5], William H.[5], Nettie[5] and Lulu May[5].

f. Barbara Jane[4] Ebersole/Eversole
born in 1826 at Caledonia, Washington County, Missouri. She died in 1920, presumably in Missouri [in 1880 she was residing at Agency, Buchanan County, Missouri]. She, age 14, married Solomon[6] Turpin on November 12, 1840, presumably at Caledonia, Washington County, Missouri. He was born circa 1818 in Garland County, Kentucky. He died circa 1875 in Missouri. His father was Daniel[5] [Hezikiah[4], Henry[3] {of Henrico County, Virginia}, Matthew[2], Michael[1] {of Yorkshire, England}] Turpin of Virginia. His mother was Elizabeth Campbell of Kentucky. Barbara[4] and Solomon[6] had three children: Daniel Thaddeus[7], William[7] and Jane E.[7]

ADDENDA PAGE

Pg Ref #   Comment/Correction/Addition/Etc.

_____

_____

_____

_____

_____

_____

_____

_____

_____

_____

_____

_____

_____

_____

_____

_____

www.ingramcontent.com/pod-product-compliance
Lightning Source LLC
Chambersburg PA
CBHW030430290526
45786CB00001B/226